I Would
Die 4 U

I Would Die 4 U

Why Prince Became an Icon

Touré

ATRIA PAPERBACK

New York London Toronto Sydney New Delhi

ATRIA
PAPERBACK

An Imprint of Simon & Schuster, Inc.
1230 Avenue of the Americas
New York, NY 10020

First Atria Paperback edition October 2019

ATRIA PAPERBACK and colophon are trademarks of Simon & Schuster, Inc.

For information about special discounts for bulk purchases,
please contact Simon & Schuster Special Sales at 1-866-506-1949
or business@simonandschuster.com.

The Simon & Schuster Speakers Bureau can bring authors to your live event.
For more information or to book an event, contact the Simon & Schuster Speakers Bureau
at 1-866-248-3049 or visit our website at www.simonspeakers.com.

Designed by Maura Fadden Rosenthal

Manufactured in the United States of America

10   9   8   7   6   5   4   3   2   1

The Library of Congress has catalogued the hardcover edition as follows:
Touré, 1971–
    I would die 4 u / Touré.
       p. cm.
    Includes bibliographical references and index.
    1. Prince. 2. Rock musicians—United States—Biography. I. Title. II.
       Title: I would die for you.
    ML420.P974T68 2013
    781.66092—dc23
    [B]
                                    2012036623

ISBN 978-1-4767-0549-1
ISBN 978-1-4767-3740-9 (pbk)
ISBN 978-1-4767-0554-5 (ebook)

Contents

"Dearly beloved,
we are gathered here today
to get through this thing
called life."

—PRINCE

Introduction

IMAGINE A FIELD THE SIZE OF AMERICA. The field is filled with people. They represent all the people who care about American popular culture, people who feel American popular culture speaks to them and helps shape and define their lives. In the middle of the field is a stage the size of Nebraska. Many people are on the stage dancing and singing and rhyming and acting and saying, "Look at me!" These people represent stars in American popular culture. Then, someone comes strolling through the field toward the stage holding a large, open umbrella, even though it's not raining. As this person walks onto the stage, the audience wonders, "Why is he holding an umbrella? It's not raining." A moment later, it begins to rain. The rain represents the feelings of the people in the audience—their dreams, fears, anxieties, and longings. It adds up to the ethos of the generation. The rain is the Zeitgeist. And the person who had the umbrella open before the rain is an icon. That person knew what the generation was feeling before they really knew, before they were able to fully articulate their feelings. When the icon takes their place on the stage they don't say,

"Look at me!" They say, "When you look at me, you'll also be looking at you."

Stars entertain us. Icons do something much more. They embody
us. They tell us something about who we are and who we want to be.
They are both a mirror and a shaping force. *Zeitgeist* is German for the
spirit of the times, the general cultural, intellectual, and political climate within a nation, or a specific group, in a particular period. You
could call it the collective consciousness of a given people at a certain
time. Icons can see and feel the Zeitgeist of their generation more
clearly than the rest of us. They have the antennae, the sensitivity, and
the intellect to become a thermometer of their era, and they have the
talent to reflect the Zeitgeist through their art. For generation X, one
of those icons was Prince.

There are truths about the soul of a generation that icons can see, as if
they're mystics, because they have vision and because they're immersed
in the culture. They are in the clubs and the bars and on the streets
and they have their antennae up and they're picking up signals about
what's going on in the world faster and more clearly than everyone
around them. This not a skill that can be taught. It's extraordinarily
difficult to make statements that will resonate deeply with several million people in your generation, but that's what icons do. They are not
only mirrors, showing the generation who they are: they are connec-
tors, bringing together a giant tribe, and sometimes they are sculp-
tors, inspiring the generation to become something. Prince rose in
the 1980s to become the mirror, connector, and sculptor of a generation, and he knew it. In 1998, I interviewed him for a cover story for

Icon magazine and asked, "Do you realize you've changed a generation with your music?" Prince became defensive. His body stiffened. The thought of it was too much. "I don't think about that," he snapped. "Why would I? There's no gain in that. Being in control of someone's thoughts? You'll second-guess your writing." He didn't see the value in being conscious of his influence, but he didn't deny that it was true.

Of course, it takes more than antennae to become an icon. Prince developed every skill that would make him become a rock star. He learned how to write timeless songs in a range of genres with masterful construction. (Questlove, the drummer for the Roots who has worked with Prince, says Prince's best albums were built with the dramatic structure of Shakespearean plays: rising action, comic relief, climax, and denouement.) He could sing in a unique, spellbinding way. He could play music in an unforgettable way; he was not just a guitar virtuoso but the master of many other instruments including drums, percussion, bass, keyboards, and synthesizer. He could dance in his own compelling style. He could perform with a rare intensity, and demonstrated a stage generalship that outshone all of his contemporaries except, perhaps, Michael Jackson. He had presence and was spine-tinglingly sexy if you were inclined to be attracted to him and, even if you weren't, he still seemed devastatingly cool. He conveyed a sense of mystery, and had an ineffability about him that left you unable to fully sum him up or feel as though you really knew him, keeping you intrigued. All this was powered by a superhuman work ethic. He knew the importance of sweat equity as a kid. In *Possessed: The Rise and Fall of Prince* by Alex Hahn, a cousin reports that Prince as a young teenager told him, "I'm going to practice my behind off like James Brown's band, and I'm going to have everything so tight that you're not going to be able to say anything about it."[1] He would grow up to be constantly working. His ex-wife Mayte once told London's *Daily Mail*, "Being with him was like being at the centre of a twenty-four-hour creative machine. If we weren't on stage, we were rehearsing. If we weren't rehearsing, we were in the studio." That's why Prince, for a long time, put out an album per year while most artists were releasing one every two years, and Michael Jackson once every four years, like a president. These are albums he wrote, produced, and played most or all of the instruments on. He was legendary for working day and night, an inexhaustible music monster. As he says in "All the Critics Love U In New York": "Body don't wanna quit. Gotta get another hit."

Several people told me Prince often worked sessions that lasted twenty-four or even thirty-six hours. Chuck Zwicky, one of his engineers, told me, "I've always admired the diligence and discipline that Prince has and his work ethic. He just kept going and kept working until he had it. I've had more than one forty hour day with him. Pretty intense. He's extremely hard working and, much to the chagrin of women, he'd rather spend his time working on his music than hanging out in a club." Zwicky said that Prince's time in the studio was almost always spent efficiently, moving at a rapid pace compared to his music-business peers. "He never spent an inordinate amount of time on one song," Zwicky said. "I've worked with artists who will agonize over a single song for many, many days. I've never seen Prince do that. He's got a very, very clear idea in his head about what the song needs to do, what it needs to sound like and he could get through it very quickly. So, typically, a session started with three written songs and ended with three completely mixed songs. He never second guesses himself and he never scratches his head. He never says, I wonder if this is good or not?"

Alan Leeds, who was from 1983 to 1992 Prince's tour manager and vice president of Paisley Park Records, said, "This is a guy who has studio diarrhea. Like you go to an office every day from nine to five, well, he goes to the studio every day. What am I gonna do today?

Well, I wrote these lyrics last night in bed so I'll make up a song. Then, he'll sit with that song and say does it fit with what I've been doing? If it doesn't, then it gets thrown in the vault. But he's constantly, constantly creating songs. So, for every song on *Purple Rain*, there's probably thirty or forty or fifty that didn't make the cut because they just didn't fit." Zwicky once told the *Minneapolis Star Tribune*, "He was so prolific, by the time he released an album, he may have had literally ten albums sitting around."[2]

Prince studied all sorts of music. Eric Leeds, Alan's brother, who played saxophone in his band on tour and during the recording of *Parade, Sign "O" The Times, The Black Album*, and *LoveSexy*, said, "Prince was quite a historian of music and could listen to something and suck up the essence of it." Associates recalled him doing a dead-on impression of Elvis, quoting obscure Bootsy Collins songs, and listening to Culture Club. Susan Rogers, who was Prince's recording engineer and maintenance tech for five years spanning from *Purple Rain* to *Sign "O" The Times* and is now an associate professor in the department of music production and engineering at the Berklee College of Music, said, "He was a big fan of Culture Club, but you got the sense he wasn't playing it for enjoyment's sake, he played it over and over as a student of the game. A scholar." A former girlfriend said he also loved Miles Davis, John Coltrane, Erykah Badu, Stevie Wonder, Joni Mitchell, and Mozart. "He thinks he could've been him in a past life. He draws a lot of parallels between himself and Mozart." She told me that, at one point, *Amadeus* was Prince's favorite movie.

In early interviews, when asked about influences, Prince pointed to Carlos Santana, Joni Mitchell, and James Brown, who he said he danced with onstage as a child. But, surely, he was also influenced by Sly Stone, Curtis Mayfield, Miles Davis, George Clinton, Rick James, Chuck Berry, Little Richard, Jackie Wilson, Jerry Lee Lewis,

the Beatles, Earth Wind & Fire, David Bowie, Mick Jagger, Elvis, and
Jimi Hendrix. Zwicky named others as well. "When he sits down at
the drums he hears Dave Garibaldi (Tower of Power). When he plays
his guitar parts, he's thinking about James Brown's guitarists (Jimmy
Nolen and Catfish Collins); those guys had the definitive funk chord
approach to the guitar. When he plays the bass, he's thinking like Larry
Graham (Sly and the Family Stone). When he's at the keyboards, he's
either thinking like a horn section or like Gary Numan. And singing
wise, I mean, there's a ton of influences. The most beautiful thing with
Prince's vocals is when he does his background vocals. You listen to
any one of those tracks on its own and it's a totally different personality singing. Together it conveys sense of the group singing. These days,
if the lead singer sings the background parts it doesn't really sound as
big because everybody's inflecting and speaking in the exact same way.
With Prince you literally felt like you were, for lack of a better analogy,
in a church and there's six people around you. Some can sing better
than others and they all have obvious personalities to them. But when
you put it all together, those six voices sound bigger than twenty tracks
of one voice. So, like, he's got this band in his head of all these unique
individual musicians. But the sum of it is Prince music. It doesn't
sound like obviously influenced."

Part of why Prince was so knowledgeable at such a young age is
because he was able to soak in sonic information at an extraordinary
rate. "One of his chief strengths was his ability to observe, assimilate
and then reinterpret," said Dez Dickerson, who played guitar with
Prince from 1979 to 1983. "So, with every engineer he worked with,
he was observing and assimilating recording techniques. He was also
observing and assimilating songwriting techniques and stuff that was
freely happening inside the band. And all of that influenced him and
he became a shape-shifter—he became great at assimilating these tech-

niques and reinterpreting them in a way people didn't recognize. And that became the genius of Prince." He also bolstered his musical education in the mid-eighties, after *Purple Rain* was released, by inviting the people close to him to introduce him to sounds they loved. In *Possessed*, Alex Hahn writes, "that led to Wendy and Lisa playing him the Beatles, the Rolling Stones and Led Zeppelin while Eric and Alan Leeds played him Miles Davis, Duke Ellington and Charles Mingus."[3]

Far from being bogged down by influences, Prince created his own genre, which mixed soul, funk, rock and pop and allowed him to be daringly innovative. Questlove said, "Prince is probably the only artist who got to live the dream of constant innovation. He pushed the boundaries with rhythm and structure and chords that no artist has ever done. He knew the balance between innovation and America's digestive system. He's the only artist who was able to, basically, feed babies the most elaborate of foods that you would never give a child and know exactly how to break down the portions so they could digest it. I mean, 'When Doves Cry' is probably the most radical song of the first five years of the 1980s because there's no bass. You don't strip down pop music. It's supposed to be full orchestration. I heard the version of 'Doves Cry' with a bassline. It wouldn't have grabbed me. Without bass it had a desperate, cold feeling to it. It made you concentrate on his voice. The narration of the song is dealing with, 'Why am I the way I am?' and it's important that you let the words paint the scenario and with the bass line you could get lost. It was distracting. With the bassline, the song was cool. Without it, it was astounding."

Prince also removed the bassline from "Kiss." He put backwards drums on "Starfish and Coffee." He omitted the hi-hat cymbal in "It." He used a method called *vary speed*, which is basically him singing or playing with the tape sped up or slowed down, to get the high-pitched guitar solo on "Erotic City" and the female-sounding voice for his alter ego Camille, which he used on "Shockadelica," "If I Was Your Girl-friend," "Feel U Up," "Strange Relationship," and others. Those songs were part of the scrapped 1986 album called *Camille*.

Questlove also told me Prince had a unique ability to program the LinnDrum machine in a way that makes it sound and feel as though a human is playing drums. "He's always adding fills and rolls that are way beyond the four-bar monotonous programming stuff of 1980s music. He's smart enough to program little things that only drummers notice. He'd purposely speed things up during the chorus and slow it down during the verse just to make you think a real drummer's playing. He was able to take the LinnDrum machine and humanize it. He established the drum machine as the bass and not the drummer and created a sound with drums that you'd never heard before. To my ears, Prince is, bar none, the best drum programmer of all time. I'll put Prince up against my favorite hiphop drum programmers. He is the master." Questlove also pointed out that Prince often mixed programming and human percussion on the same song, for example, on "Lady Cab Driver" he gave us a live snare and a programmed kick and hi-hat. On "Automatic" there's live cymbals and a programmed kick and snare.

Prince wrote great, timeless pop songs because he understood what was sonically essential. "There are so many popular records that don't contain great songs," said Susan Rogers. "If you strip them down no one is going to sit down and learn the chord changes. But Prince was a strong enough songwriter that you could strip his songs down to just the skeleton and you'd have something pretty valid there. You'd have good lyric writing, in some cases great, and you'd have strong melodies. And on top of that he was able to add harmonic progressions that were innovative and smart. Underneath that he was able to add a rhythmic foundation that was great. He taught me that you should be able to strip out everything except the bass and drums and maybe one rhythm instrument and it should sound like a record. He was so smart, he truly understood how each piece needs to function. It's rare for music makers to really understand that." Rogers said Prince also understood how to use all of the major ways to make songs connect with listeners. "I'm a psychologist," she said. "I know that there are three avenues through which listeners can bond with a piece of music. There's our motor system—music can make us move. There's our emotional system—even something without drums in it can move us. Just chord changes alone can move us emotionally. And there is our cognitive system—lyrics can make us think. If you're a genius at any one of those you don't need to be that good at anything else. So, in other words, James Brown makes you move, even if you don't understand English. Those who are geniuses with melody and can write a great chord change will make us feel. Those who are geniuses at lyrics, whether it's Bob Dylan or Bob Marley, will make us think. Prince understood those three avenues. He knew that he had three ways to connect with people and, unlike most of the artists I've ever worked with, he aimed to be a master at all three. Very few artists are that strong."

Of course, Prince's innovative sound was difficult for some people to understand. Zwicky said, "A friend of mine, who was dating him back in the era of *1999* and *Purple Rain*, said people would just walk right up to him and confront him about his music saying, 'What kind of music is that you're doing? It's not rock, it's not funk. What is this?' Well, he was doing what he liked to hear."

Prince also developed into a bandleader who knew just how to push the musicians who worked with him past their capabilities, and bring things out of people that they didn't know they could do. Eric Leeds said, "This is the kinda guy who had the ability to walk in a room and instantaneously present a musical vision. He could get us together and all of a sudden realize something that was on a rarified level. I really enjoyed going in the recording studio with him. It wasn't about whether or not the song we were working on was something I would want to go home and listen to. That's not why I was there. I was there because he was very good at being able to reach inside you and bring things out of you that wouldn't naturally be what I'd end up doing myself." Prince accomplished that by motivating people in particular ways. Eric said, "One time, in a recording session, he told me I want you to play a solo on this song but I want you to approach it as if you just picked up the saxophone for the first day in your life. And being a huge fan of Miles Davis I related it to the same thing Miles used to tell Herbie Hancock and Wayne Shorter and Tony Williams. He said, I don't pay you to play for me what you know. I pay you to play for me what you don't know. And I would try to look at it in the same way. And those are the experiences that I treasure. But most of the time it wasn't about what he would say but about creating that vibe. He did it in a very personal way. I worked with George Clinton on several recordings. George would create the same kind of environment but George, not being a player, was like an alchemist. He would get everybody in a room and set up a vibe and get something out of you like that. Prince was an instrumentalist, so he was more hands on, but they would both set a vibe."

It takes more than a wide array of talents to become a generational icon; part of why Prince became one is that his oeuvre dealt with what is perhaps one of the ultimate questions: Can we have both reverence for God and fulfill the rawest of carnal desires? Can the spiritual imperative and the lustful urge co-exist in one soul? Prince had much to say on the issues of the irrepressible sexual impulse and our innate spiritual needs, as well as apathy in the face of the apocalypse. His messages fit generation X. He was talented, yes, but, crucially, he lived a life that uniquely prepared him to understand the gen X experience and wrote songs that spoke to the things we cared about—our desires, our fears, our longings, our anxieties—and that is why he became a generational icon.

1

Prince's Rosebud

Prince was born in 1958, so he is a baby boomer. However, he did not demand boomers learn a new cultural language in order to understand him, as Run-DMC and Nirvana would. Prince validated their musical taste and knowledge, which they appreciated, just as Adele succeeds, in part, because of an older audience that remembers 1960s soul, or Lady Gaga, partly because of an audience that fondly recalls Madonna. But boomers do not make up the majority of Prince's audience, simply because they were a bit too old when he hit his stride. Many gen Xers were in their teens and early twenties during the period of Prince's largest commercial and cultural success—from 1983's *1999* to 1992's *Symbol*. During that time, the vast majority of boomers were over thirty and, after the age of thirty, most people stop being obsessed with pop culture in the way that those between fifteen and twenty-five often are. Music is constructed for and driven by that age range: fifteen-to-twenty-five-year-olds are more likely to buy albums, concert tickets, and merchandise because, for them, musical icons often become part of their way of shaping or expressing who they are or who they want to be. Sociologists say people aged fifteen to twenty-five are in active identity formation mode, as opposed to thirty-somethings, who have a stronger sense of self and look to popular culture far less to help express and shape themselves.

Cultural icons also aid peer bonding among teens and emerging adults (people in their early and mid-twenties). Part of why we like certain artists is that we like the other people who like them, we enjoy being associated with or attached to those people, we want to be in a tribe with them. After thirty, that social transaction is less valuable, largely because the most important tribe for that point becomes the family and/or work community. Of course, that doesn't mean that all people over thirty shun popular music, they certainly don't, but the majority of Prince's audience during his commercial and cultural peak were the gen Xers, for whom he was like a knowing big brother helping them define who they want to be in the world. He was just old enough to know the sixties and just young enough to understand gen X. Even given his prodigious talent, had Prince launched his message in a different time, it would've have been received differently, because it would have fallen on ears sculpted by divergent experiences, and shaped by dissimilar worldviews. Prince and gen X clicked on a deep level because they were made for each other.

Steven Van Zandt from Bruce Springsteen's E Street Band once told me, "Nothing is inevitable." He meant no artist is so talented and no song is so perfectly written or sung that you can just put out that artist or that song and watch people gravitate to it like bees to flowers. It always takes more than talent: Entertainment isn't a meritocracy. Van Zandt was making an argument about the necessity and importance of managers in music. He said the Beatles would still be in Germany and the Stones would have been playing dinner theaters, if not for great, visionary managers who helped sell them to the world. The same can be said for generations. No icon is so talented that they don't need the right generation to receive their message. Of course, some icons transcend their time, but that's nearly impossible without first connecting deeply with the generation that's consuming culture when you're at your peak. The difference between being famous and becoming an icon is, in part, having the good fortune to have a generation that's interested in your message.

We can get a glimpse of how Prince might have been received by many boomers from the response he got when he opened for the Rolling Stones in Los Angeles at the Memorial Coliseum on Friday, October 9, and Sunday, October 11, 1981, during the *Dirty Mind* era: He got booed off the stage. Twice. Matt Fink played in those shows. "Mick Jagger and Keith Richards were enamored with Prince," Fink recalled, "and they felt he was someone who should be introduced to a huge audience, so they requested his presence as a warm-up act. It was after *Dirty Mind*, going into *Controversy*, and they wanted to give his career a boost and introduce him to mainstream rock-and-roll fans and people in their circle of fans. So, we were brought on board to perform at two shows at the Los Angeles Coliseum. Ninety thousand people, sold out. The lineup was The J. Geils Band, then Prince, then George Thorogood and the Destroyers, and then the Stones." This must have been a huge compliment to Prince, who thought a lot about Mick in the early days. Dez Dickerson said, "The one thing he talked to me about a number of times in the early going was he wanted he and I to be the Black version of the Glimmer Twins. To have that Keith and Mick thing and have a rock 'n' roll vibe fronting this new kind of band. That's what he wanted."

Fink recalled: "We went on when the sun was still up, I think we hit the stage around six or seven at night, we were supposed to do a half hour or forty-minute set, tops. We get on stage and within two minutes of the first song the audience, which was a hardcore hippie crowd, they took one look at Prince and went what the heck is this? And they started booing, flipping us the bird, I'd say out of the first sixty rows of people, 80 percent of them were flipping us the bird. And they're throwing whatever they could get their hands on. So, here we are being pummeled with food. I got hit in the side of my head with a crumpled up Coca-Cola can. I saw a fifth of Jack Daniels whiz by Prince's face; must've missed his face by less than a quarter of an inch. That scared the bejeezus out of him and three songs into his set he walked off stage in a bit of a panic, some fear going on there. And he did not signal us to stop playing, he just walked away and left us there, so Dez had to signal the band and get us to leave the stage. After we got off the stage there was some confusion and we said where did Prince go? They said he took off. He got in the car and he left. He flew back to Minneapolis and made the decision not to continue on with any more shows with the Rolling Stones." Ironically, Prince walked off during "Why You Wanna Treat Me So Bad?" which clearly had a different meaning that night. Jagger called Prince and begged him to come back and do the Sunday show. There was a lot at stake—there were several more shows scheduled in other markets. Jagger told Kurt Loder of *Rolling Stone*, "I talked to Prince on the phone after he got cans thrown at him in L.A. He said he didn't want to do any more shows. God, I got thousands of bottles and cans thrown at me. Every kind of debris. I told him, if you get to be a really big headliner, you have to be prepared for people to throw bottles at you in the night. Prepared to die!"[1] Dickerson told Prince he'd played in racist biker bars and had been attacked even worse. He told Prince, "You can't let them run you out of town." Prince flew back to Los Angeles for the Sunday night show. It did not go better.

Once again, bottles and food were thrown. Dickerson recalls a bag of old, smelly chicken pieces flying at the stage. It was obvious the audience had contempt for the funky little man who dressed androgynously and sated too little of their macho-rock needs. Prince told Robert Hillburn of the *Los Angeles Times*, "I'm sure wearing underwear and a trench coat didn't help matters but if you throw trash at anybody, it's because you weren't trained right at home." He was incensed by the scene. "There was this one dude right in front and you could see the hatred all over his face," Prince told the *Los Angeles Times*. "The reason I left was because I didn't want to play anymore. I just wanted to fight. I was really angry." Fink recalled, "Prince said, 'This is absurd. Why should we put up with that? Those are people who've grown up with the Rolling Stones and just look at my image in a multiracial group and me in my high heels and thigh-high stockings, bikini briefs, no shirt and a trench coat. This is enraging them and I'm not going to put up with it." Fortunately, for history, he didn't need to. Perhaps if Prince had arrived ten years earlier, or if we could somehow put him in a time machine and release him in a previous period, maybe he would've gotten that same cold response from other audiences. Maybe he would've been only as big as Rick James instead of becoming one of the seminal figures of his time. Maybe, as Van Zandt would say, he wouldn't have made it out of Minneapolis. Maybe.

In *Outliers*, Malcolm Gladwell talks about how success is always tied to good historical timing. One example he cites is Bill Gates, who grew up at a moment when there were very few computers in society. However, there was one at his high school. He was able to put in over

10,000 hours of practice and learn how to code at a high level, thus putting him in perfect position to capitalize as personal computers became ubiquitous. Being born at that specific transitional moment in the history of computers—when he was one of the few who had access as a kid, and one of the few who had early expertise as an adult—is not something Gates controlled. It was good historical timing. That stroke of luck plus his prodigious talent led to him become a technology supernova. If he'd been born just five years earlier or later the outcome might have been different. Timing matters. Being in the right moment matters.

Gladwell could have given us the example of Michael Jackson, who was also the beneficiary of good historical fortune. As a child, Jackson was signed by Motown, which exposed him to the best imaginable music school with teachers like Diana Ross, Stevie Wonder, Marvin Gaye, Suzanne De Passe, and label founder and president Berry Gordy. When Jackson began his solo career in 1979, he did so just before the launch of MTV in 1981 and the introduction of the compact disc in 1982. At first, MTV played white rock artists almost exclusively but, over time, they bent to pressure from many sources to include Black music. Jackson's second solo album, *Thriller*, arrived at the end of 1982, and was perfectly timed to become the first album by a Black artist that MTV embraced at a time when the nation was starting to transition to an exciting new sonic format called the CD. There were lots of yuppies (young urban professionals) and buppies (Black urban professionals), that is, twenty-somethings and thirty-somethings with good jobs who were flush with cash and eager to spend it. The middle class was exploding with people who'd grown up watching Jackson, and now found him making hot new music packaged on a hot new format, being lionized by a hot new music-centric TV station on which his incredibly ambitious short films played. No one in history had ever had such an amazing confluence of awesome talent, first-rate teaching, and the good fortune to unleash a great album in a strong economy while a cool, new format was being introduced and an influential new medium was captivating us. That perfect storm led to the biggest-selling album in the history of music, and it happened in large part because of several factors Jackson did not control.

When I speak of Prince's good historical timing, what does that mean? Well, before we can understand how Prince fit so snugly within the culture of generation X, we have to unpack what that culture was. What was the Zeitgeist of the world that Prince meshed with in order to become an icon? What was the cultural weather for gen X?

When we speak of gen X, we mean people born approximately between 1965 and 1982. As of this writing, gen Xers range in age from early thirties to mid-forties. I sit toward the early middle of the group, born in 1971. People born before us, born between about 1946 and 1964, are called baby boomers. They're now in their late forties to mid sixties. People born between about 1983 and 2001 are considered millenials or echo boomers or the net gen or gen Y. As of now, they are late preteen to late twenties. People born after 2001 are, so far, called gen Z. I'm sure that will change once they begin to assert their generational personality.

That said, these generational borders are not hard borders; they're soft ones. Nothing magical happened between 1982 and 1983 that makes people born in those years so radically different that they must be in different camps. Researchers disagree a little on the specific years demarcating each generation, and far less on the spirit of each one. When we move away from the edge years and into the heart of the time periods, we find people whose feelings, expectations, and values are shaped by being inside the time markers of their generation. People who are in similar phases of life tend to find themselves brought together and shaped by the major historical events, social trends, technological leaps, and cultural touchstones of their time.

The size of each generation has had a huge impact on its character. The generation before the boomers, called the silent generation or the lucky few, had about 40 million people. Then, the victorious soldiers of World War II came home and found economic opportunity and widespread optimism about America's future, which led to an explosion of births and the baby boomer generation swelled to 80 million. The massive size of the boomer generation forced America to change in response to a large influx of people, at a time of boundless American efficacy led the boomers to think they could and should change the world. If it seems that boomer needs and memories continue dominating America and the sixties remains a present part of modern culture, as if it were a kid still sitting there in the high-school cafeteria reliving the golden days when he was young and popular, even though he graduated from college years ago, well, that's partly because there's so many boomers in America.

In 1965, the birthrate began to fall and the generation that emerged, gen X, would end up being about 46 million people. Sociologists think the smaller size of generation X is partly because of the pill becoming widely available in the sixties and the legalization of abortion and the sharp rise in the number of working women in the seventies. In the early eighties, the birthrate began rising again, marking the beginning of the millenials, or the echo boomers, who would swell to number about 78 million. The boomers have continued their outsized impact on America by having a truckload of children. Meanwhile, the smaller size of gen X defines us, sometimes making us feel like a squeezed out middle child, overshadowed by the boomers and their romantically turbulent 1960s, and the tech-savvy millenials in a world forever changed by the Internet.

Still, demographics are an imprecise tool for nailing down the intra-generational connections we're talking about. People do not match their generation simply because they're born within a given range of years. A more precise way of delineating people is through *psychograph-ics*, which means classifying people by psychological criteria like atti-tudes, fears, values, aspirations, and the cultural touchstones that mean the most to them. Looking at things through a psychographic lens allows people to be a bit more self-selective about which generational groups they fit in, and provides a sharper reasoning for why people are considered part of certain generational groups and not others, as well as why some people may share traits of two generations and why the borders between generations are soft. To get at the psychographics of generations we must explore the incidents and institutions that impact each generation. These are the signposts for the generation, or the seeds for the weather of a given generation, the things that happened to shape the shared ethos, feelings, and values of its members.

The incidents and institutions that a generation experiences en masse become the generational touchstones that bring them together and shape how its members feel about the world. For the boomers, some of the most seminal events that reflect and shape their genera-tional character are Woodstock, the Vietnam War, and the assassina-tions of John F. Kennedy and Dr. Martin Luther King, Jr. These were moments that interacted with and challenged that generation's sense of immense optimism and hope that they could unite and change the world, and they struggled to deal with them. For millenials, 9/11 was a life-changing moment that reshaped their world and taught them that America was no longer a safe place and launched a long period of dis-trust and fear that we still have not emerged from. The so-called great recession of the late 2000s and early 2010s has also marked milleni-als, launching the national Occupy movement, saddling millions with college debt and useless degrees, as well as forcing millions to live with their parents into their mid- to late twenties, delaying their ability to start careers and families. Also, everything millenials do, and the way they think, has been molded by the Internet in general and by social media in particular, as well as by texting, interconnectivity, and the pervasive ADD that comes from perpetual multitasking.

What was the seminal event for gen X? When I started writing this graf I wasn't sure, even though I lived through it. After considerable research, I felt the truly epiphanic event for gen X was not any public event but instead one private event that happened to so many of us, that its impact reverberated onto those who didn't experience it directly. For gen X, the seminal event that binds the generation and shapes and defines who we are and what we will become is divorce.

When generation X was young, divorce became far more common than it had been for boomers or would be for millenials. In 1960, a few years before gen X was born, there were under ten divorces per 1,000 married women. In the 1970s this number skyrockets and, by 1980, when gen Xers range from young teens to babies, it peaks at over 22 divorces per 1,000 married women. After that, as we move into the birth of millenials, the trend declines to around 16 per 1,000 by 2009. In the 1970s and 1980s, divorce touched one million children per year.

For many young people, divorce is akin to an apocalypse. It is not a death in the family, but the death of a family. It changes their world forever and causes permanent damage. The way you look at family changes, the way you love changes, and the way you go about your day-to-day activities changes, because of new family arrangements and being beholden to two homes, and/or to single parenting, and/or remarriage, and/or blended families, and so on. Divorce can create emotional ruptures that will never heal, thus fueling much of the cynicism, skepticism, disillusionment, nihilism, and distrust of traditional values and institutions that marks gen X.

So many gen Xers experienced divorce that even if your parents never divorced, you were still impacted by the abstract specter of divorce or the concrete realities of other families changing. There's a constellation of ways in which divorce impacts people and, like a mushroom cloud, they extend to people who aren't in the divorcing families. The divorce of others might rock your certainty that your nuclear family will be together permanently. Also, the issues that arise because one teen's parents have suffered a divorce—from depression to the use or abuse of drugs to many other things—can easily spill over and impact their peers. For example, the parents of a member of my high-school peer group went through a nasty divorce, which led to them battling for his love by buying him things and giving him privileges that none of the rest of us could dream of enjoying. He had a car two years before the rest of us did, thanks to his dad. This facilitated us acquiring alcohol on weekends, which his mother allowed us to drink at her house without supervision. There's no easy way to measure how his feelings about divorce and his pessimism about marriage infected us. With millions of gen Xers internalizing so many feelings stemming from divorce, there's no way that can fail to impact their peers. People often experience the breakup of couples who are close to them in traumatic ways. For young people still figuring out who they are, the divorce of people in families near them can have a large impact. In the legendary film *Citizen Kane,* a reporter tries to get to the essence of the life of Charles Foster Kane by searching for the meaning of the last word Kane says on his deathbed: "Rosebud," which symbolizes the key, buried element that will help you understand the soul of a person. Well, divorce is the Rosebud of both gen X and Prince.

John Lewis Nelson, the grandson of slaves, was born in Louisiana in
1916 and moved to Minneapolis in his thirties. He became a plastic
molder at Honeywell Computers, as well as a pianist who led a jazz
band called the Prince Rogers Trio. Prince Rogers was his stage name.
In 1956, at a show in Minneapolis, he met a jazz singer named Mattie Della Shaw, who was about sixteen years younger than him. Shaw
grew up in Baton Rouge, Louisiana, and moved to the projects in
Minneapolis, where she and her twin sister, Edna Mae, developed a
fearsome reputation on the basketball court. She became the singer
in Nelson's band, but quit after becoming his wife in 1957. Nelson
already had four children from a previous marriage, and, in 1958,
the year Prince was born, Nelson had a son, named Duane Nelson,
with another woman. Two years later, Prince's parents had a daughter,
named Tika, also called Tyka. Soon after, their relationship began falling apart. In 1965, when Prince was around seven years old, his parents formally separated.

In 1981, Prince told *Newsday* that his father "felt hurt that he
never got his break [as a musician] because of having the wife and
kids and stuff. [Mattie] knew that and there were constant fights. She
could see a lot of that coming out in me and used to say that to me a
lot." In a 1996 interview on *The Oprah Winfrey Show*, Prince said his
father had abusive moments, and that the most autobiographical scene
in *Purple Rain* was "probably the scene with me looking at my mother
crying,"[2] which happens as a result of her being hit by Prince's father.
After his parents' divorce, Prince lived with his mother, but many say
the time he spent in her house was rocky because she was easing into
a relationship with a man named Hayward Baker, whom she would

marry in 1967. Prince once told a reporter, "I disliked him immediately."[3] At some point, Prince was forced out of his mother's house, possibly because of Baker's feelings about her son and, according to some, because Baker was abusive or violent toward him. It's whispered that Baker may have beaten Prince or locked him in a closet for some period of time. Prince may be referring to this obliquely in the 1996 song "Papa," in which a four-year-old is pushed into a closet by his father, who then shuts the door. "As the door closes, baby starts to cry. Please don't lock me up again, without a reason why." Later in the song he says, "Don't abuse children, or else they turn out like me."

The Reverend Art Erickson, who knew Prince as a child, said to biographer Jon Bream in *Prince: Inside the Purple Reign*, "He told me a story once about how his stepfather locked him in his room for six weeks and wouldn't let him out and the only thing in there was a bed and a piano, so he learned to play the piano. Personally, I think a lot of his background feeds into his life."[4] Susan Rogers said Prince told her he was abused as a child. Others claim Prince exaggerated these stories from his childhood (locked in a room for six weeks?) in order to make himself seem more enigmatic or sympathetic or deep or take your pick.

Prince spoke with Chris Rock about when he lived in his mother's home in their 1998 VH1 interview. It's one of the rare times he mentioned his mother in the media and it's impossible to know if he was being honest or if he was exaggerating and myth making. He said, "Once my mother remarried it was a period in my life where she had to teach me about the birds and the bees and I think, I've never asked her about this, but there was some sort of plan to initiate me heavy and quick. So I was given *Playboy* magazines and there was erotic literature laying around and it was very easily picked up and it was pretty heavy at the time. I think it really affected my sexuality a great deal."[5] In 1983, Prince told *Rock & Soul* magazine the same story with a slight difference: "My mother used to keep a lot of pornographic material in her bedroom and I used to sneak in there and read it. This had a great deal to do with my sexuality today." [6]

People who have known Prince say he has been shaped by his difficult relationship with his mother. "There were issues between him and his mom," Dickerson said. "He didn't talk about them a lot and I got the sense that part of why the focus was on his career was because he put that stuff in the rear-view mirror." Eric Leeds told me, "He spoke of his mom very, very, very rarely. That was a subject that you never wanted to bring up to Prince. It was a sore spot with him. You knew not to bring it up. It was not a secret that he harbored a lot of resentment toward his mother." Everyone I spoke to said that Prince discussed his mother rarely or never. Within the Prince camp, all knew it was a sensitive subject to be avoided.

After leaving—or being kicked out of—his mother's home, Prince, still a preteen, went to live with his father. According to Zwicky, Nelson spent some of his time playing music at a strip club in downtown Minneapolis. Stories vary as to how Prince eventually came to leave his father's home: He may have run away or he may have been thrown out by Nelson. Some say Prince was caught at home with girls, others say Nelson felt his young son was getting in the way of his skirt chasing. Bernadette Anderson, who would become a surrogate mother, told Dave Hill, author of *Prince: A Pop Life*, "It was after the [Grand Central] band had played somewhere the night before, and his dad got mad at him and put him out. Some girl had followed him home and she'd stayed there. Prince said 'I didn't do anything wrong, but I can't explain that to Dad.' His dad was very strict." [7] There's a legendary story about Prince calling his sister Tyka from a pay phone and begging her to ask their father to take him back in. She called and spoke to Nelson, then called Prince to say he should call him. Prince did, but Nelson still refused to let him come back. Prince crumbled into tears and vowed to never cry again. Or so the story goes.

Prince spent his teenage years bouncing around Minneapolis. In a 1981 *Rolling Stone* interview he said, "I ran away from home when I was twelve. I've changed address in Minneapolis thirty-two times, and there was a great deal of loneliness. But when I think about it, I know I'm here for a purpose, and I don't worry about it so much." In 1984 he told *Rock* magazine, "From my Dad's, I ran to my aunt's. Then back to my Dad's, then to a [foster] home."[8] In 1984 Prince told *People*, "I was constantly running from family to family. It was nice on one hand, because I always had a new family, but I didn't like being shuffled around. I was a bitter kid for a while, but I adjusted." Not only was he a child of divorce but he was also a latchkey kid.

Being a latchkey kid is another way Prince was linked to a seminal gen X experience. There was a rash of gen Xers who were latchkey kids because of divorce or two-career families, due to the explosion of women in the workforce in the seventies and eighties. Studies say as many as 40 percent of young gen Xers were latchkey kids, meaning they had more free time than any generation in American history. They often lacked parental guidance in the hours after school and had to care for themselves or other family members. Out of that lack of supervision came independence, individualism, resilience, self-reliance, adaptability, and an entrepreneurial spirit, as well as forays into drugs, alcohol, crime, sex, or suicide attempts. Generation X, in its early years, had a high suicide rate.

Prince ended up living in the basement of the home of Bernadette Anderson, mother of his friend Andre, whom he would later hire to play in the earliest versions of the Revolution under the name Andre Cymone. Some say that, for a time, Prince looked at Bernadette as if she were his mother. She seems to have been permissive and supportive of his musical obsession. Prince and Andre often jammed in the basement and apparently the music never really stopped. In 1984, Bernadette told *Ebony*, "The cutoff time for music was ten each night and

sometimes I'd lie there and hear Prince's stereo cut down real low and
he'd be playing his guitar. It never bothered me though." Still, as much
as he considered her like a mother, he kept his emotional distance. In
1984, Bernadette told *People* magazine Prince "didn't get too close to
people. He never talked about his mother and father.He kept a lot feelings to himself."[9] Bernadette gets one cameo in Prince's oeuvre. On
"The Sacrifice of Victor" from the *Symbol* album he says, "Bernadette's
a lady and she told me, 'Whatever u do son, a little discipline is what
u need, is what u need, u need to sacrifice.'" She gets a compliment, or
perhaps a royal title, and gives him advice that he clearly took to heart;
the value of sacrifice is at the heart of the song. When Prince mentions
his mother in his songs, he is never that sweet.

At some point, before *Purple Rain*, Prince welcomed his father
back into his life. Susan Rogers said, "When I worked for him, his
relationship with his father was good. They had reached some kind
of resolve and some kind of peace." Zwicky said things weren't always
good. "With his father, Prince was the mean one in that relationship,"
he told me. "I've seen him throw his father out of the studio for simple
things." Prince and his father worked on music together and Nelson is
co-credited on several songs, including "Computer Blue," "Around the
World In A Day," "The Ladder," "Christopher Tracy's Parade," "Under
the Cherry Moon," and "Scandalous," a period that spans from *Purple Rain* to *Batman*. Many people tell stories of Nelson hanging with
Prince in Minneapolis or on tour with the Revolution in the 1980s.
Alan Leeds told *Wax Poetics* magazine, "Father and son couldn't boast
of a warm, fuzzy history but Prince seemed bent on making up for lost
time. John attended all of his son's major events and sure didn't mind
his entrée to rock star creature comforts, including the companionship
of a cutie who had been a popular Playboy model."[10]

A 1984 *Ebony* story mentions Prince giving his father a purple BMW and taking him for rides on his motorcycle. "We're great together," Nelson says. "He has a photographic mind and remembers a lot about me and my music from his childhood. Of course, he's young and I'm old, so we can't be buddies, but we usually talk about music."[11] A 1985 *Rolling Stone* story about Prince co-stars Nelson, who's driving around Minneapolis with Prince and playing pool with him. "Prince peeks in the rearview mirror," the story says. "John Nelson is still right behind. 'It's real hard for my father to show emotion,' says Prince, heading onto the highway. He never says, 'I love you,' and when we hug or something, we bang our heads together like in some Charlie Chaplin movie. But a while ago, he was telling me how I always had to be careful. My father told me, 'If anything happens to you, I'm gone.' All I thought at first was that it was a real nice thing to say. But then I thought about it for a while and realized something. That was my father's way of saying, 'I love you.'"[12]

Eric Leeds said that later in Nelson's life he and Prince fell out for good. "I knew John," Eric told me. "After Prince reconciled with his father there were quite a few years where they were close. But it's my understanding that there had been another falling out between him and his father and I don't believe it had been reconciled by the time his father passed away. I believe his father in his last years was experiencing quite a degree of dementia and Prince is not the kind of person who likes to be around that. Those kinds of things are very difficult for him to be able to emotionally process." John Nelson died in 2001, at the age of eighty-five.

It's said that Prince did not attend his father's funeral.

The relationship pattern Prince had with his father—becoming famous, then embracing him, then later rejecting him—seems to have been repeated with his half-brother Duane, who was a foot taller and the source of the "Lady Cab Driver" line: "This is why I wasn't born like my brother, handsome and tall." Prince and Duane went to the same high school and were in the same grade. After Prince became a star, he hired Duane to work at Paisley Park as a security guard. That lasted for twelve years. Zwicky said, "Duane was a couple feet taller than Prince and a simpleton himself. He lacked the edge. He was much more happy-go-lucky." For some reason, Prince fired Duane and filed a restraining order against him. People from Minneapolis say Duane fell on hard times financially and physically, before he died in 2011 at the age of fifty-two.

By all accounts, there was never a moment of reconciliation between Prince and his mother. The portrait of her that emerges from his songs and interviews is rather devastating. This seems to fit with a gen X pattern, whereby boomers usually spoke of their mothers with saintly reverence; in the ultraconfessional world of gen X it was not uncommon for Mom to be blamed as the source of your troubles.

Mattie Shaw is a spectral presence in the Prince story, rarely mentioned and less often seen, conspicuous through her absence. It's poetically fitting that, in the 1985 *Rolling Stone* story that co-stars his father, Prince drives past his mother's house but doesn't stop to see her. " 'That's where my mom lives,' he says nonchalantly, nodding toward a neatly trimmed house and lawn. 'My parents live very close by each other but they don't talk. My mom's the wild side of me; she's like that all the time. My dad's real serene; it takes the music to get him going. My father and me, we're one and the same.' A wry laugh. 'He's a little sick, just like I am.'"[13] Note how Mom got a brief mention, then Prince segued into talking about his dad, likening the two of them, discussing his bond with his father and, by being silent about his mom, underscoring his lack of connection with her.

Many think Prince's failed relationship with his mother led to him becoming a control freak who's obsessively self-reliant and untrusting of anyone. Alan Leeds said, "If you can't trust your mother, who can you trust? That's the template for his life. Shit, I couldn't trust her, so I'm gonna trust you? So, he never completely trusted anybody." Alan Leeds began working with Prince in 1983, when the star was twenty-five years old, and he could see Prince was troubled. "The person I met," he said, "was suspicious and paranoid of people and life in general and sarcastic and cynical and clearly troubled by his personal demons. And of course the more we learned about his background the more we learned why he wasn't a very secure individual—his mother basically walked away from him. And his father struggled to raise him and threw in the towel. The kinds of rejection he suffered as a youngster certainly don't add up to a very secure, well-rounded individual." The familial rupture led to Prince becoming a person who cannot trust others, and must be in dictatorial control of everything around him, Leeds explained, "Anyone assuming any kind of control frightens the hell out of him. So much of what he does is driven by fear, fear of someone else having control."

Susan Rogers told me that Prince's maternal void was something she could relate to. "Losing his mother was tough," she said. "One of the things that I think kept the two of us together and made us sympathetic to one another was that my mother died after a long battle with cancer when I was a kid and I left home very early, at seventeen. And that was something that we recognized in each other. When we related to each other, we related as young people in search of healing, in search of something that would make us right and that would give us what we didn't have. We knew that about each other and it kept us together for a long time."

Still, some sort of relationship between Prince and his mother was retained into adulthood. In *Prince: A Pop Life*, Dave Hill wrote that Shaw "would call Mrs. Anderson from time to time to make sure Prince was going to school. Today she introduces Mrs. Anderson to people as 'Prince's other mother.'"[14] Alan Leeds said, "I met her a few times. Prince would invite her to events, Minneapolis concerts, holiday parties he'd sometimes throw for the band and friends, and his birthday parties. When she showed up it was usually with her second husband, which Prince reluctantly tolerated. But I never noticed anything suggesting any normal mother–son intimacy." She showed up at the Hollywood premiere of *Purple Rain* in 1984 and told a reporter, "I can't believe all the stars!"[15] (Eddie Murphy and Christopher Reeve were there.) In the late eighties, Prince bought her a home in Minneapolis, according to the *Minneapolis Star Tribune*. In 1996, she was at Prince's first wedding. And, in 2001, when John Nelson passed away, she attended the funeral.

After Prince left her home, Mattie went on to earn a master's in social work from the University of Minnesota and spent over two decades as a social worker in the Minneapolis public-school system. Tyka once told Jon Bream of the *Minneapolis Star Tribune*, "She loved working with children."[16] After Mattie's death, a co-worker named Wayne Jensen told Bream she was great when making home visits. "One time there was a parent actually drinking mouthwash," Bream wrote. "She confronted the parent about how they were taking care of their student. I've never seen anyone like her who could, in a tactful way, talk about caring for their child."[17] Baker died in 2002, at the age of sixty-eight. Prince is said to have skipped her funeral just as he had skipped his father's. The night she died he performed in Chicago and told the crowd she had "made her transition." In her honor he played what he said was her favorite song of his, "Anna Stesia."

Prince's mother comes up in only three of his songs that I could determine: "When Doves Cry," "Another Lonely Christmas," and "Extralovable" (also called "Xtralovable"), a 1982 song that wasn't officially released until 2011. The portrait of her in these songs is not flattering. He describes her as "never satisfied" (on "Doves Cry"), unable to be pleased or impossible to get approval from. She's also called "as straight as straight can be" (on "Extralovable"), which I read as her being unapologetically rigid. And in "Another Lonely Christmas" Prince gets in a sardonic dig as he cries over a dead girlfriend: "My mama used 2 say, always trust your lover. Now I guess that only applies 2 her." He seems to be referring to her trust in her second husband.

I suspect that the chorus of "Doves Cry" may be Prince addressing his mother. Alan and Eric Leeds agreed. When Prince says, "How could you just leave me standing, alone in a world that's so cold?" that is a question he may have wanted to put to his mother who, he feels, abandoned him. Yes, it's possible that he may be addressing the question to both his parents; when Prince called his father from a pay phone, begging him to take him back in, according to the legend, it was raining, which means Nelson literally left him standing alone in a cold world. But I think Prince was speaking to his mother when he wrote those lyrics because, by then, he had reconnected with his father and, according to so many, the rupture of his relationship with his mother seems to have rocked him much more deeply. I also believe that because of the way Prince answers the question, "How could you just leave me standing, alone in a world that's so cold?" He blames himself and likens himself to the person who helped drive his mother away: "Maybe I'm just too demanding. Maybe I'm just like my father, too bold." This sounds to me like Prince speaking to his mother, asking how she could be so heartless and searching for reasons why. If he's just like his father then it makes sense that she would abandon both of them. This could also be Prince speaking to a lover with whom he has a complicated and difficult relationship—despite them having great sex as described in the verses.

"Doves Cry" could also be addressed to both his mother and his lover; some people echo the relationship they have with their opposite sex parent in their romantic relationships. Which perhaps explains why he likens his mom and his lover, "Maybe you're just like my mother. She's never satisfied." The song seems to be the ultimate bizarre relationship song with its two verses that speak in detail about lust and intercourse and then the chorus, which seems so alien to the verses that it may be the subterranean familial history still living inside Prince that explains his relationships. The pain of his parents' troubles and the complexity of their differences are scars that sit inside him and possibly explain why we scream at each other even though we have great sex. This, even though he wants peace, wants to be a dove, but ends up crying because relationships are so painful. For a generation raised on divorce, this opaque musical poem about the complexity of difficult relationships was catnip.

At some point in his teens, Prince decided the way to solve or escape his familial problems and personal demons was to turn himself into a rock star. The pain of divorce and the freedom of latchkeyness propelled him. Alan Leeds told me, "He was the guy who was always in the music room practicing piano when everyone else was outside because he sat down as a youngster and designed himself to be a rock star. Not a musician, but a rock star. There was an acceptance and power and security that he envisioned could come from massive appeal. Here's how I can get back at the world. Here's how I can get the girls and be the number-one guy and get the attention that I never get. Because this is a guy who grew up with issues. He had mother and father issues. He had small-man complex. He was the shortest kid in school. He had light-skinned issues. He was the obnoxious, nerdy guy in school. Nobody liked him. He was ostracized. Guys picked on him because his mama left him and his dad wasn't capable of being a serious father. He was an excellent basketball player but nobody took him seriously because he was too short. He was constantly in the shadow of everybody and everything."

Many people dream of being rock stars, but Dez Dickerson said there was something special about Prince that allowed him to chase that dream. "What he was at a DNA level made it possible for him to create himself as a rock star more effectively than another kid who had the desire to do it but didn't have the tools to pull it off. There was insight that he had, there was intellect that he had, that not everybody had." He was also blessed with far more free space than the vast majority of teens around him because he was a functional orphan. He was living in Bernadette Anderson's home at the time when, as a divorcee with six children, she was pursuing a degree at the University of Minnesota, so Prince probably lacked the supervision that most children have, giving him the uncommon power to shape his own life. He also had an unusual amount of willpower, which he used to mold himself. Prince's high-school band director James Hamilton once told *People* magazine, "A lot of boys had more talent than Prince. The difference was his determination." [18]

Susan Rogers saw the full extent of Prince's will after she finished working with him and went to Los Angeles to work with the Jacksons on the album that became *2300 Jackson Street*. She stayed at the family compound and talked a lot with most of the Jackson brothers (not Michael) about their early lives. "It was so interesting and moving," she said, "that [the Jacksons] arrived at this place of fame and the top of the music charts as did Prince but their lives were so completely opposite. Prince was totally a self-made man and the Jacksons, especially Michael, were born, bred, groomed, prepared, honed, shaped, and molded to become what they became. Prince did his by a singular force of will coupled with the talent."

In his high-school days, Prince was constantly playing music in the school music room. A 2004 article in the *Minneapolis Star Tribune* by Jon Tevlin said, "Football players coming in from practice could hear him banging on the piano or the guitar, hours after other students had gone home. During lunch hours, the music teachers locked the door for him so he could practice without interruption." People said he would sit in the hallways and play his guitar long after the final bell had rung. Prince had always been drawn to music, but it was also a way for him to prove himself. Eric Leeds said, "[Playing music] is the only conduit via which he could establish any self-esteem or value. And he had a very high degree of emotional neediness in that regard." Prince's high-school web site says, "While attending Central he was very active in music, taking as many of these classes as possible. He was a member of the sophomore basketball team and he showed off his talent at the many talent shows. Prince didn't pay much attention to his academic subjects because, he thought, he didn't need to because he was going to be a star."

Prince didn't just dream of stardom but immersed himself in the business of music class. "He was in it for all three years he was there [at Central]," said the teacher, James Hamilton, to Dave Hill in *Prince: A Pop Life*. The class covered contracts, copyrights, demo tapes, and more, which Hamilton had learned working with Ray Charles. "It was letting them become aware that you can't just stroll into this world and become a star." Apparently, Prince's plan was to do just that, and he told Hamilton, "I'm trying to be as controversial as possible. I have to get people to buy the records." Hamilton told Hill that Prince's greatest asset was his work ethic and the intensity with which he practiced.[19]

In his teenage years, Prince developed his self-reliance and his entrepreneurial sense and mastered a variety of instruments rapidly. He taught himself to play and write music. In his first interview, a 1976 talk with his high-school newspaper, he said that he plays by ear. "I've had about two lessons," he said, "but they didn't help much. I think you'll always be able to do what your ear tells you." He said he liked his music teachers because they let him work on his own.

At thirteen, before Prince was legally old enough to get into a club, he often played at Minneapolis's First Avenue as part of a band that was at first called Grand Central and, later, Champagne, which had Morris Day on drums. Prince soon grabbed the attention of everyone in Minneapolis who cared about music. "I heard about him in the wind around town," Dickerson said. "He had stepped into that urban legend status of, hey have you heard about this kid? That there was this kid in Minneapolis who was like the new Stevie Wonder, who played all these instruments." Those who had not yet heard about him because of his musical ability surely heard about him when, at the age of seventeen, he shocked the Minneapolis music scene by winning a three-album record deal for what was rumored to be over $1 million. He earned that, and an unusual amount of creative control, because he had not just been studying music and learning to play, write, produce, and engineer, but he had also studied the business of music.

When Dickerson auditioned for nineteen-year-old Prince he immediately felt Prince was "Mature beyond his years. He didn't say much but when he did speak there was a depth coming out of his words that you didn't see with cats that age. And he had a look on his face and in his eyes that you could tell this dude is thinking nonstop. And then when we stepped outside to the parking lot he asked me some very mature, career-minded questions." Perhaps typical of someone with such an unconventional upbringing, even though Prince was extremely mature in some ways, he remained immature in others: He never developed the basic social skills and the ability to be comfortable with people.

Zwicky told me that people who knew him in high school looked at the superstar Prince and said, "When did he get that personality implant?" In high school, he was an introvert and a loner. He had his picture omitted from the school yearbook in his junior and senior year, symbolic of his inability, or lack of interest, in connecting with people. Susan Rogers said she once read Prince's high-school report cards after his mother came by and dropped off a box of his childhood things, which was the only time Rogers ever saw her. Rogers said, "I went through his report cards and I looked at the comments that his teachers wrote about him and they wrote about the same guy that I knew, the guy who was sitting there next to me. He's quiet, he's respectful, he's polite, he's obviously very bright, but he kept himself apart from the other kids for the most part. He was incredibly shy." A high-school friend, Paul Mitchell, once told an interviewer, "A lot of people felt sorry for him. He would get on people's nerves sometimes. I think it was just his frustration lashing out at people. I think he was trying to be cute and get attention. He didn't get it at home. I think at times he had to feel left out because he just didn't have anyone. But he never talked about the family problems, even to Duane." [20]

By all accounts, young Prince was very quiet and low-key. A 2004 *Minneapolis Star Tribune* story about Prince's high-school days quoted a basketball coach saying, "He was so shy, you couldn't believe it to see him perform in front of people. He never said anything in class. But he is one of those students everybody talks about." [21] That may have something to do with his sense of style: The *Star Tribune* story said he often wore "an open shirt with large collars, maybe a pair of baggies over platform shoes, and a choker around his neck. His hair was teased into an enormous dome that Buckminster Fuller would envy, and his upper lip wore a faint moustache. Sometimes he had an Afro that made him look six feet tall. Other times he wore cornrows."

The Reverend Art Erickson, who knew Prince as a teenager, told Jon Bream in *Prince: Inside the Purple Reign*, "In high school, he retreated into himself quite a bit—he would eat lunch alone and he became very reflective. The divorce, a lot of things, hurt Prince. And out of that hurt probably comes a lot of his expressions today—a lot of anticulture, antifamily, antiestablishment, antiinstitutional feelings."

Prince's difficulty relating to people in small groups or one on one has followed him into adulthood. "He doesn't have normal relationships," Alan Leeds said. "It's not like he's got guys that he hangs out with on Friday night. He's not one for small talk or casual conversation. He's so strictly defined by his career that there really hasn't been a normal life away from that. Demonstrative, but it's all superficial. He's not a person who finds it easy to share, whether it's his thoughts or his time or his energy. If it isn't within the context of a specific purpose he doesn't enjoy or solicit sharing life. Everything has an agenda." Leeds said every once in a while Prince would cancel the almost-constant rehearsals in favor of a cookout and some hoops or some other sports bonding event. "Once," Leeds said, "we were rehearsing for a tour and suddenly there was the first warm day of the year and when everybody showed up for rehearsal we found out that Prince and his assistant had bought ten baseball gloves, a couple softballs, a couple bats, and we went to the local school field and played softball all day. But, in the midst of that, he's constantly talking about the last record he did and the tour we're gonna do and what should we do tomorrow in rehearsal. That function never ends. He's a very distant personality. Prince isn't close to anybody. He's a very, very emotionally aloof person. I don't know anybody who's ever gotten past that wall." Despite how confessional Prince's music seems, even his fans have not truly gotten past that wall. For example, take the story of "Wally."

Among the most serious Princeologists, the song "Wally" is discussed in awestruck, reverential tones as if it were the Holy Grail of the Prince catalog, the one song that would finally allow us to know the deepest, most pained level of him that he has never truly shared. Alas, it's a song that will never again be heard. Only two people ever heard the original version: Prince and the engineer of the song, Susan Rogers. "I can tell you about Wally," Rogers said. "This is the part that I'm really reluctant to talk about because I've spoken about his personal life and I've regretted it and the only way I could justify it in my own right is to say, well Susan, it's okay to speak about your personal life because it was my life, I was there. So I'm not going to try to read anything into his head but I'll tell you what I saw. He had a long relationship with Susannah Melvoin, where it looked like they were going to get engaged."

A source told me that they sort of got engaged—Prince gave her a ring but may not have viewed it as an engagement. He gave her the ring just before they departed for Nice, France, to shoot *Under the Cherry Moon*, and though she showed it off to people—"gleefully"—neither Prince nor Susannah used the word engagement to describe their situation. The day after Prince and his team arrived in Nice for a three-month stay, a source said, "he suddenly and inexplicably sent her back to the states." They remained a couple but she could see he wasn't ready to commit—just days after she left France, Sheila E. was staying in his house. Susan Rogers encountered Prince at a moment when the relationship with Melvoin was definitely over.

"It was on and it was off and finally it was off and it was off for good," Rogers said. "She was gone and I knew, I assumed, that it was hurting him pretty badly 'cause this was a really deep on-again, off-again relationship and now it was over and it was completely over. His behavior changed. He started wearing different clothes and he had a different look. Changing things. I expected that there would be a song that would reflect how he was feeling. I was wondering when it was going to come." It came on December 26, 1986. "We were in Minneapolis and this was a Sunday and it was wintertime, there was snow on the ground, and he called me to his house to record. So, I went over and it was just the two of us. I put up a roll of fresh tape and he played every instrument. This was not uncommon. He would play the drums and then play the piano and the bass and strings and things and eventually he would do the vocal and I would leave the room so he could do the vocal by himself and then I'd come back in and mix it. So, I came back in and I heard the vocal. It was called Wally, and he starts by speaking to Wally Safford [a bodyguard and then a singer and dancer on the *Sign "O" The Times* tour]. It's a monologue and he's saying, Wally, those glasses are really cool, can I try them on, 'cause I'm going to a party and I want to look clean. So, he tries on the glasses and he says this is great and then he says, I want to look good 'cause I hope I meet someone. I hope I meet someone because my woman left me and then it goes into the chorus and the melody was just beautiful, he's a genius with melody, and the words of the chorus are, 'oh my la de da, oh my la de la, my la de da, oh my melody and oh my malady, my sickness, oh my la de la . . . ' It was beautiful. All based on piano but with a lot of strings and at the end the music breaks down, and he hands the glasses back to Wally and he says, keep these glasses, I don't need them now, I'm going home, something to that effect. So, we finished it and we spent the whole day, just the two of us, tracking everything and mixing it. I thought it was the greatest thing he had done. I had waited years to hear a Prince song like that. I ached to hear him be so honest. There was so much pain in that song. It was heartrending. He said, 'Do you know that *maladie* means sickness in French? It's almost like the word melody.' He was getting all this pain out." But, at some point, Prince began to change the song, ruining its heartfelt sentiment by adding percussion and making it more funky. Rogers tried to stop him. "I said, 'Don't you think it was better before? Maybe we should stop.' But he was destroying it deliberately. It was just too honest. Then, he looked at me and he pointed to the multitrack and he said, 'Now erase it.' And I said, 'What? Excuse me?' He said, 'Put all twenty-four tracks in record and erase it.' He'd never done anything like this before and it was one of the best things I'd ever heard him do. I said, 'You've got to be kidding me.' And he said, 'If you don't, I will.' And I said, 'Please will you just think about it? Can we just put the tape away and just think about it overnight? I'll do it tomorrow if you still want it done.' He steps towards the machine and he put all twenty-four tracks in ready record and he hit record and he wiped the whole thing and he took the cassettes." She paused, perhaps still slightly pained by the memory of the beautiful aborted song. "It was confessional," she said. "It was close to the bone. He was saying this is what I'm feeling, I feel terrible. Most artists would have seen that as their ticket to stardom, that kind of vulnerability, that kind of . . . honesty. But every artist gets to manipulate the degree of honesty that they're willing to show. It's boring for people to confess too much. It's smart to hold something back. In that case, I thought he held too much back. I thought he would have been more likable had people known who he was, had they known the person I knew. The guy was hurting. It's okay to hurt but he didn't want people to know that."

Prince, as she said, never made anything quite that beautiful and honest and harrowing and he never erased anything else, either—as Zwicky said, this was an artist who never second-guessed himself—but in the case of "Wally" it was too much to share. "Music is a vehicle for self-expression," Rogers said, "but the artist gets to decide how much of himself he wants to share with the public. This was an instance where music writing was a vehicle for self-expression that he chose not to share. He rarely employed it but that was one time when he did."

Many said Prince has tried to soothe the pain of being unable to truly connect with people—and the ache of lacking a traditional nuclear family—by turning his bands into his family. In 1984, Wendy Melvoin, a seminal guitarist in the Revolution and twin sister of his girlfriend, Susannah, told *People*, "We're more than a band. We're definitely Prince's family. We're always hugging and comforting each other." [22] However, it's relevant to note that in 1986, not long after she said that to *People*, she quit, came back, then was fired, which is perhaps indicative of how it's hard for Prince to make his bands into functional family units because he has so little experience with nuclear families. Matt Fink said the rift Prince had with Wendy and her girl-friend Lisa Coleman, a crucial keyboardist in the Revolution, boiled down to money and respect. "I think he wasn't paying them for some session of work they thought they were owed," he said, "and he was also having them work long hours and having them at his beck and call twenty-four/seven. He would call them at three a.m. and say get down to the studio and they wanted to go back home and be in LA and they felt they were being held hostage almost." Alan Leeds said the problem lay in Prince repeatedly begging the girls to move to Minne-apolis permanently, rather than staying in a hotel and keeping their roots in Los Angeles. The ladies resisted and the failure of that effort, as well as stress from Prince's relationship with Wendy's twin sister, added to the tension and, one day, a silly issue at rehearsal became something larger and Prince fined Wendy for some infraction. She refused to pay, an argument ensued, and that's when Wendy and Lisa quit. They were talked out of quitting before they finished packing their things—by Alan—and they went through with a planned European tour but, according to Leeds, "Prince didn't make any real effort to make a last-ing peace. He just wanted to get through the tour." At the end of the tour, he fired them.

Because it's Prince, and because the professional breakup with Wendy and Lisa was seminal, the end of an era in Prince's career, there are no shortage of explanations as to why they were fired and what it says about Prince. "He's got separation issues," Eric Leeds explained. "If you're gonna leave him he has problems with that. He hates to be left. That was really the reason why he fired Wendy and Lisa. They had made it known to him that they were considering leaving the group and his reaction to that was he couldn't allow himself to go through what was for him going to be emotional trauma particularly for two people that he felt a certain artistic closeness to. Closer artistically with them than with anybody he's ever had in any of his bands. The emotional trauma that I think he realized he was gonna go through if they were to leave him made him say I have to do this preemptively. I'll be damned if I'm gonna allow them to walk out on me. I'm gonna fire them. And that's what he did." It may sound like a dysfunctional family but it surely does not sound like the sort of fulfilling family unit Prince seemed to want from his band.

Eric Leeds told me, "Prince always looked at his band as being his family but he did not know how to express those feelings or have those relationships in a normal sense. So, he became so obsessively possessive about it and it wasn't that he wanted us to be his band as much as he wanted us to be his cult of personality. It always had to be one sided. He wanted the love and devotion that we were supposed to give him, but it was not necessary for him to return it if it didn't suit his purpose. Normally, you look at a relationship and it's based on a give and take. A relationship is dynamic in that both people get to have a turn controlling the relationship. But Prince is obsessed with always controlling the relationship entirely. When he's not in a position where he knows he can control the relationship, he just removes himself from the relationship. Life to him is a movie in which he's the director, the producer, the screenwriter, the casting director, and he's the star. And everybody else in his orbit is a character in his movie." Susan Rogers called him the most Machiavellian person she had ever known.

Gayle Chapman, who played keyboards in the Revolution from 1979 to 1980, said Prince struggled to communicate with band members and understand how to be a band leader. "He was still working on himself," Chapman said. "The way he handled certain issues, things that, in my opinion, are really simple, to just talk about, constantly became big. But Prince got to the point where he didn't talk to me about personal issues cause he was so lousy at it." When Prince was unhappy with what Chapman was choosing to wear onstage he struggled to explain that to her. "Prince came to my door and was really

upset with me, and told me that he would fire me if I didn't do something different. And I said, okay, fine, I'll do something. No big deal.
All you got to do is say something. Then he sent his girlfriend down-
stairs with a bag, a paper bag, and she reiterated that I had to wear
this, or I was fired. I opened the bag and it was multicolored metallic
underwear and a bra that were clearly the wrong size for me. I looked
at it and I put my fist in the cups of the bra, and said, 'Hey, Mary, first
of all, this is a C cup; surely you understand this. But I think I know
what he wants, so I'll go shopping. Tell him not to worry. I'll get him
something that he wants.' So, I went to a local lingerie shop and told
the owner of the shop what I was doing and why I was there and he
locked the doors and started racking up stuff and I was there for like
an hour and a half, drinking wine and trying on stuff. That night I
didn't reveal what I was wearing until we walked up on stage, where
I took off a robe, and revealed this new outfit. I tossed the robe, and
the guys, while the crowd is screaming about us coming onstage, the
band is not paying attention to the audience, they're paying attention
to, holy shit, Gayle!"

Chapman said at some point Prince instituted a rule about how
the band was to dress any time they were in public: The members of
the Revolution were to dress like rock stars whenever they went out
for any reason. She said, "If you walk out of your hotel room you were
supposed to be in your rock-and-roll garb. Spandex. Naked. Hair.
Whatever. Full make-up and spandex just to get razor blades at the
hotel shop. You never left your room not looking like you were ready
for work. I'd get so many stares. They thought I was a hooker. But
he was building an image and not just for himself. Now, we all know
that rock stars actually dress in blue jeans and t-shirts like the rest of
us sometimes but back then it was like, we were on the road, and we
always had to look the part." Again, the guy who wanted his band to

be his family wasn't treating the band like family, but using them as extensions of himself.

Eric Leeds said at one point Prince wanted the band to all be vegan. Alan told his brother that to survive being in Prince's band you had to at least pretend to drink the Kool-Aid, so, Eric said, you had guys being vegan when Prince was around and eating whatever they wanted when he wasn't around. "He attached some spiritual component to it but looked at it as another way for him to exercise control," Eric said. "If you're gonna work for me then you have to conform to my ideal."

Becoming a rock star did not tame the demons inside Prince that arose from his childhood having been ripped apart by divorce and shaped by functional orphanhood. Asked what he thought of Prince as a man, Eric Leeds said, "There's a degree of tragedy there because this is a guy who after all the success and legitimate and remarkable achievements which are the result of his talent, hard work, discipline, and focus, and after all that he still looks at himself as a victim. And it kind of pisses me off because I don't think he has a right to look at himself as a victim. There are people who go through that and some-how find peace with it, regardless of whether they ever reconcile with their mother. They just make peace with it and decide this is the hand I was dealt but I've got a huge life in front of me and it doesn't make sense to let this completely define or limit what my life is gonna be like. That's not him."

Prince's highly abnormal childhood was spent learning how to inter-act with instruments more than with people as he made a conscious climb toward becoming a rock star. In the Central High graduation program, Prince had his future employment listed as music. With all that practicing and working in bands and studying the music business and sometimes sleeping in a recording studio, he seems to have been sort of a man-child with the music part of his mind highly developed while the interpersonal part of his personality remained malnourished. "This is a kid who was never allowed to have a childhood," Eric Leeds said. That statement brings to mind Michael Jackson, who began performing at eight, signed with Motown at ten, became a star at eleven, and never stopped working. That, as we have seen, can be corrosive. The other biggest name in pop music in the eighties was Madonna, who had a normal childhood—compared to Prince and Michael Jackson—although she was shaped by having lost her mother to breast cancer when she was five. Prince's mother did not die, but in practice, he lost her. So where Jackson and Madonna each suffered one painful trauma—losing a childhood or losing a mother—Prince, in his own way, suffered both of their traumas. One would be enough to stunt a personal's emotional development.

Eric Leeds said, "This is a guy who has done some exceedingly generous and thoughtful things for me and other people but then a day later he could turn around and say something so off the wall and so ridiculously stupid and you'd say how do I reconcile these behaviors? People would wonder is he a bad guy who has good days or a good guy who has bad days? I think it's because he has the emotional maturity of a five-year-old. And he never understood the value of doing something thoughtful for somebody on its own merits. He really didn't understand the consequences of him doing something nice for somebody any more than he gave importance to the consequences of him doing something really nasty to somebody. The child doesn't know that yet. You teach your child what works and what doesn't and establish how relationships work. Well, Prince never got that and, to this day, he never has."

A former girlfriend echoed that sentiment. "He seemed tormented. He was tormented. That's for sure. He was struggling with this duality of good and evil. Sometimes, you'd get happy, fun Prince but more often you'd get complicated and heavy, almost like he was performing around me when it was unnecessary. There were times when I would see him, the essence of who he really was, if he was sleepy. Then he was funny, down to earth, sweet and insecure, and clearly not performing. But, if he was awake, he was on, guarded about showing too much of himself or he didn't think it was worth his time. He didn't think it was significant enough to try that hard. He didn't try that hard to give anyone clarification about himself or what he was going through."

Professional success has not cured Prince's interpersonal problems, it's just given him the space to not have to say sorry. Eric Leeds told a story that he said would encompass the brilliance and the lameness of Prince and how his difficulties relating to people can frustrate even his biggest cheerleaders. "Here's the dichotomy of Prince," he said. "In 2004, at the Rock and Roll Hall of Fame induction ceremony there was a tribute to George Harrison. A performance where Prince got onstage and performed with a whole bunch of rock 'n' roll guitar players, icons." It was Tom Petty, Jeff Lynne, Steve Winwood, George's son Dhani Harrison, and Prince who performed "While My Guitar Gently Weeps." Leeds continued, "It was not something that Prince would typically do, i.e., allow himself to be part of someone else's agenda musically. But after they all did the song and played a little solo and Prince was the last one to solo and as soon as Prince started playing you could see the look on the other guys' faces: We only hold this instrument; this guy actually plays it. Because, in thirty-two bars of music Prince just wiped the stage. It was so unaffected and natural and I said, Go ahead, Prince! Because that's the Prince that I relate to. The exceptional musician. I said, Prince did it again. My man! As soon as the song was over, all the other guys put their arms around each other to celebrate that they'd done this performance in honor of George Harrison. Everyone except Prince. He threw down the guitar, looked at the audience dismissively, turned around, and walked off. Here you have this wonderful performance where he steals the show and you wanna say, go ahead Prince! That's still the baddest motherfucker out there! And what does he leave you with? Oh, my God, is this guy an asshole."

Prince tried to create families at home, too. He was engaged to Susannah Melvoin (in 1985) and married to Mayte Garcia (in 1996) and Manuela Testolini (in 2001). His efforts to create a lasting family have been either cursed by his lack of experience or stymied by horrific luck. A former-girlfriend told me, "He has great respect for women. And a blatant disrespect and disregard for women. Not when he's speaking to you, but in his actions. They're not genuine. He's not honest. He's not a good husband. He gets bored easily. He's not monogamous. He's very controlling. And he's not that sweet to them."

In 2006, Mayte told England's *Daily Mail*, "I wasn't allowed to call him, ever. Even when we were married; I had to wait for him to call me. I've no idea why, he never actually said . . . It was a strange relationship." I visited Paisley Park in 1998, when Prince and Mayte were married. There was a child's jungle gym out back that looked as if it had never been used. It was put there in anticipation of a child after Mayte became pregnant in 1996. Prince sampled the baby's heartbeat for a song on *Emancipation*. However, in October of that year, when Mayte gave birth to the child, named Boy Gregory, he had Pfeiffer syndrome, a skull deformity. After seven days on life support, he died. In 2012, on VH1's *Hollywood Exes*, Mayte said, "I had him to term. I held him. He lived for a week. It's hard to have that life inside of you and it not continue. It's still really hard. I still think about him." Prince has said that "Comeback," a ballad from his 1997 acoustic album, *The Truth*, part of the Crystal Ball set, is about the child: "Spirits come and spirits go. Some stick around for the after show. I don't have to say I miss you. Cuz I think you already know." The refrain is, "If you ever lose someone dear to you, never say the words they're gone. They'll come back."

The truth about this moment may be a little different than we've been told. A source told me that a Minneapolis pediatrician said that Prince and Mayte actually gave birth to twins. Both babies had severe problems and didn't survive. "Prince went over the deep end after that," said someone who knew him. "He had a really difficult time dealing with the grief and the anger about the situation." Susan Rogers was no longer working with him then, but she heard that this was, understandably, a very difficult time. "From what I understand," she said, "this was really a turning point in his life." In 2006, Mayte told the *Daily Mail*, "Losing a baby is a terrible thing. Some couples are brought closer together after the loss of a child, others are driven apart; in our case, the latter happened."

These repeated failures to create fulfilling families in his band and at home, as well as the adulation and insulation that would extend from Prince's massive professional success, left him with little reason to feel he had to come out of the shell his childhood traumas put him in. So often life taught him that to connect, to trust, to let yourself need someone can easily lead to intense pain. So, why not just stay behind your mask?

I got a glimpse of Prince's weird ways of interacting with people when I spent time with him at Paisley Park for a cover story I was writing for the now-defunct *Icon* magazine. It was 1998, and we did an interview that was too short and incomprehensible to support a cover story, partly because he didn't allow recording devices, which made it nearly impossible to capture the dramatic, diversion-filled paragraphs he speaks in and that sometimes went in circles, using parables and sentences so cryptic that they'd fit in a David Lynch film. When I looked back at the notes I'd scribbled while he talked I kept asking myself, *what did that mean?* The notes I wrote did little justice to what he had said and I couldn't commit his quotes to memory due to his unique language. So, his quotes, in my story, were often approximations of what he said, usually more his intent than his exact words. Apparently, he intends to be cryptic. An former girlfriend said, "Sometimes he says things that make you feel like you haven't gotten an answer. He leaves you to have to think about every word he says, which is kind of irritating."

After our interview, I asked his publicist if I could email him more questions. Because I had a cover story to do, it was allowed. I emailed Prince ten. The last question was, "Will you play basketball with me?" (I knew that in high school the only thing he really cared about, apart from music, was basketball. He played on his high school team and by all reports he was good although his chance to get a lot of playing time was stymied by being small.) Well, one night a few days later, he emailed back answers to some of my questions and ignored others, but to my question about basketball he wrote, "Any time brother . . . :)." Any time? I put a basketball in my bag and boarded the next possible plane to Minneapolis. I don't think he expected that. I wanted a real human interaction with him but didn't know if he could or would give it to me.

Paisley Park is a large, modern-looking building located in a field just outside of Minneapolis, in tiny Chanhassen. From the outside, the large white-tiled walls make it look like a Mercedes dealership without windows. Inside Paisley, which houses recording studios, a large rehearsal stage, and offices, there was a quiet manicness, as if it's a music lover's *Alice in Wonderland*. Oversized comfy chairs of all colors sit amid pillars topped with gold disks and thick blue carpeting dotted with zodiac signs. A flock of golden doves seemed to tumble from the sky in a painting on one of the walls. (People said the building had been a clean, minimalist white for fifteen years, but had become colorful, either because of the influence of his new wife Mayte or in anticipation of a baby.)

As Prince sat for a photo shoot that would accompany my story, he spoke to us in weird but witty asides. Flipping through *Vanity Fair*, he came to an article about Ronald Reagan, long after his presidency, battling Alzheimer's.

Prince asked, "Think Reagan has Alzheimer's?"

"Yeah," I said.

He gave me a sly look as if to say, don't believe it. I'd heard he was a conspiracy theorist. I laughed and began writing what he'd said in my notepad.

"Don't write that!" he said playfully. "I'll have the Secret Service at my door." He adopts a mock federal agent voice. "You say somethin' about Reagan?"

The room cracked up. I asked, "Why would they lie about that?"

He said, "To keep him from answering questions."

When I pulled my basketball from my bag and told him I wanted to play ball he told an assistant to "clear out the back to play basketball" and get his sneakers. I'd heard he played in heels. "Who told you that?" he said in an incredulous tone, as if that were the most ridiculous suggestion ever. I said, "I don't remember." He said, "A jealous man told you that story." (Not quite: Wendy Melvoin once told the *Minneapolis Star Tribune* that Prince would sometimes break from rehearsals to play basketball . . . in heels. She said, "He would go outside and play basketball in the high heels, which he's now paying for, I'm sure. With his heels on, he could run faster than me, and I was wearing tennies.")[23]

Prince disappeared and, after a short while, the two-person photo team and I were led toward the back, into the rehearsal room. When we got there, Prince was jamming with his band while wearing a tight, almost sheer, long-sleeved black top and tight black pants. He had changed since the photo shoot only minutes before. After a few songs, he put down his guitar and walked around a corner to where there was a single basketball hoop and enough room to play half court. He slipped off his cream colored heels and reached into a box of sneakers and pulled out some old and clearly used, but not too tattered, red-and-white Nike Air Force high-tops. He laced them up and with that, the guy who was a backup point guard for Central High in Minneapolis was ready to ball.

He picked up my ball and made a face that was understood in international shit-talking parlance to mean I'ma kick yo' ass, and started knifing around the court, moving quick, dribbling fast, sliding under my arm to snatch rebounds I thought for sure I had. He was showing off, being competitive, and, yes, engaging me in the same way I'd interacted with so many men I had played basketball with before. He moved like a player and played like one of those darting little guys you have to keep your eye on every second. Blink and he's somewhere you wouldn't expect. Lose control of your dribble for a heartbeat and he's relieved you of the ball. He jitterbugged around the court like a sleek little lightning bug, so fast he'd leave a defender stranded and looking stupid if he weren't careful. With his energy and discipline it was a rapid game, but never manic, or out of control. Still, we were both rusty so most shots missed, clunking off the side of the rim or the backboard. After a while, there was not much of a score. I scored on a drive that felt too easy and as the ball dropped in I looked back at him. He said, "I don't foul guests." Okay. On the next play I drove again and the joker bumped my arm really tough, fouling me. Funny dude.

After a time he and I teamed up against my photographer (who Prince had told not to take pictures of the game) and Morris Hayes, his six-foot-four blond, Afroed keyboardist. Prince played like a natural leader, setting picks and making smart passes, showing a discipline many street players never grasp. Then, he took it boldly to the hole, twisting through the air in between both opponents to make a layup. It was, maybe, a bit too aggressive, but he exhibited the confidence of a man who's taken on the world and won.

Once, I was dribbling the ball at the top of the key when I saw he was in good position under the basket. I flicked a quick, no-look pass his way. The ball zipped past both defenders but then I realized he didn't know it was coming. I started to yell out to him, the man I had known, sort of, for over fifteen years. I called out, "Prince!" But this was during the Symbol period, when his name was unpronounceable and you weren't supposed to call him Prince. Titanic faux pas! Would he storm out and banish me from Paisley Park? I had this thought process as the word "Prince" was coming out of my mouth so really what I said was, "Pri . . . !" like the first syllable, then caught myself and slapped my hands over my dirty mouth as if to keep that sound and any other from getting out. The ball sailed past him and out of bounds. He jogged off to retrieve it and as he walked back he had a badass smirk on his face. I looked at him, like, "What?" I had no idea what would happen next. Then the man laughed as he said, "He didn't know what to call me." He loved the confusion, loved that I didn't know how to connect with him, that I was off balance and couldn't even call him by a name much less really know him. That symbolized so much. After balling and bonding and being guys together, teammates, he still relished there being a barrier between him and me, keeping us from getting close. Still, I kept trying.

A few moments later I passed to him on the baseline and, full of poise, he coolly threw up a jumper. It swished in and we won the game. He was too cool for school about it. We high-fived, but he still kept a distance. After that, we took a walk alone together through a giant closet, a warehouse-sized room filled with clothes on racks. He pointed out some past tour outfits and abruptly gave me a black-and-gold hockey jersey with his logo on the front. Then, he showed me an old picture of him playing tennis and said he was really good at the sport. He said, "I was too small to play"—he pointed back toward the basketball court—"in high school. I like tennis better than that." Finally, he was sharing with me, taking me beyond image making and toward the real man. I thought we were about to really connect for a second. I said something about playing tennis—I had a vision of somehow playing with him. Then, he abruptly excused himself in a way that made it clear that this was not goodbye. Then he was gone. An hour later I was still in the lobby of Paisley Park, waiting to keep talking or say goodbye or something. Someone came down and said it was time to go. They said that saying goodbye wasn't his way. Perhaps it would come too close to a normal human interaction.

Prince's sense of dislocation from the world was a classic trait of generation X. We are not all misanthropes, but gen Xers are famously apathetic and cynical because of the metaclimate of the world we were raised in. And not just because of the divorces all around us. The boomers grew up in a positive atmosphere: America had won World

War II, established itself as the world's leader, and as a place with a strong economy where most people who worked hard could ascend to a higher class. Thus, they were flush with efficacy and optimism that they could change the world.

The metaclimate in America during gen X's youth was marked by declining national self-esteem. We grew up in the shadow of Watergate and the Vietnam War (the first war America ever lost), we watched the Iran hostage crisis stretch on through 1979 and 1980, and we feared the potential nuclear apocalypse of the long Cold War with the Soviet Union, which seemed as powerful as America, or perhaps more so, making it difficult for us to cling to the image our parents had taken for granted. Even Henry Kissinger said that we had passed our historic high point. It appeared as though we were in the twilight of America as a dominant nation; you didn't have to be paying close attention to geopolitics to see that.

At home, in the 1970s, we had three recessions, a gas crisis, 9 percent unemployment, and the widespread expectation that gen Xers would be the first generation of Americans who would not be as well off financially as their parents. We heard that as kids and, indeed, a 2007 study said that it had turned out to be true, Gen X men made 12 percent less than their fathers did at the same age in 1974, reversing an historical trend. We watched the fortunes of the American middle class slowly decline through the 1970s and then recoiled at an historic stock market crash in 1987, that came to be called Black Monday. In the early 1990s we entered the worst job market since World War II. We inherited a nation of declining wages and shrinking job possibilities, where people worked harder for less money, and where expensive college degrees led to *McJobs*, a term that arose from gen X to signify pointless, futureless, low-paying jobs often held by overqualified people.

Gen Xers also realized as young teens that we would not get to engage in the sexual freedoms that our parents had enjoyed, because we came of age under the specter of AIDS: a time when sexuality was fraught and linked to death. When Tom Brokaw, Dan Rather, and Peter Jennings began telling us about a frighteningly fast-moving epidemic spread by sex, I was a thirteen-year-old virgin, just beginning to figure out how to get a girl to kiss me. I remember thinking, "Are you kidding me? This is the time in history I'm born into? When sex can cause death? Are you fuckin' serious?" I really thought that. I'm sure I wasn't the only person who thought that.

Meanwhile, America was being invaded by a massively powerful drug called *crack*, which made the entire drug economy far worse than it had ever been. Being addicted to crack wrecked lives faster and more completely than we'd ever seen. Both the addicts and the dealers were ruthless, violent, desperate, and spiritually lost. With crack, like divorce and AIDS and America's geopolitical status, you didn't need to be directly impacted by these things to be changed by them—you could all but feel the reverberations of their impact in the air in America. You could hear it in the stories we told about ourselves. You could see it all around you.

Where boomers had grown up in the 1960s feeling full of hope, Xers in the 1980s could not reasonably feel that way. The boomers' optimism seemed naïve and inappropriate to us. Where boomers rejoiced in 1969 over the excitement of putting a man on the moon, gen Xers in 1986 watched in horror as a space shuttle exploded, killing seven people and destroying the space mission. Where boomers watched the election of JFK and the ascension of MLK, men who inspired us to think of the boundless potential of humanity, Xers grew up with hearing about Watergate and Vietnam and never got the chance to be politically innocent. We had every right to be cynical, skeptical, sarcastic, pessimistic, nihilistic, and distrustful of the world.

The cynicism, skepticism, sarcasm, and irony remains in gen X's soul and is reflected in so many of the cultural products we love. Studies show the newsman our generation trusts most is Jon Stewart, who's a comedian doing the news while mocking media conventions—a typically gen Xish layered, nuanced, and postmodern ironic approach to media befitting a worldview that likes to see through hype. Our love of seeing through the hype and seeing things in layered ways, looking through multiple simultaneous lenses comes together in *The Matrix*, an extraordinary film that said the reality you see in front of you is not reality at all. The movie created a huge cultural explosion within gen X. Other movies have sold more tickets and DVDs, but none has had the same kind of lasting cultural impact and influence, because *The Matrix* and its central metaphor spoke so well to what gen X felt. Movies like *Reality Bites*, *Slacker*, and *Clerks* brilliantly portrayed gen X, they are movie-as-mirror, while *The Matrix* employs gen X values to drive its narrative. (A friend argued that *The Matrix* should be read as a millenial film because it's technoreligious and utopian and filled with hope. Clearly, *The Matrix* has enough cultural energy, and the right timing to speak to and belong to both generations.)

Of course, the central visual poet exploring gen X themes, our filmic poet laureate, was director John Hughes. He wrote and directed a slew of iconic films in the 1980s and 1990s about being a suburban American gen X teenager. The two Hughes films that had the largest lasting impact on culture, and expressed perfectly what it meant to be a gen Xer, are *The Breakfast* Club (1985) and *Ferris Bueller's Day Off* (1986). Gen Xers felt dislocated, apathetic, and dispassionate, which was misread by boomers, who labeled us slackers. We knew we were not slackers. Both those Hughes films show that dual sense of a world that views gen Xers are slackers while the characters, the audience, and the film itself knows better. The characters in these films are literally dislocated from society as they know it: In *The Breakfast Club*, they are spending a day trapped in detention, which is isolation, and in *Ferris Bueller's*, they abandon school, the center of their world, to go on

a journey through Chicago. Also representative of the teens' dislocation from society is that the parents in these movies are spectral, either
literally (as in, you see them minimally) or figuratively, like Bueller's
mother and father who are present but so clueless and ineffectual that
they are easily manipulated. But, in both films, the parents still matter:
Teens reveal deep-seated pain about their parents being emotionally
absent from their lives, as well as their fears about growing up to make
the mistakes that the adults around them are making. Bueller himself
is not apathetic at all, but he is cynical, sarcastic, and dislocated from
society, in that he has no regard for authority be it parents, principals,
maître d's, or parade-float managers. He's disaffected with a smile, a
rebel without a cause who's about nothing more than living in the
moment and doing whatever he wants whenever he wants without any
concern for society's rules or his own future.

A generational outsider may see these characters as slackers who
need a lesson in respecting authority—and the adult authority figures
in the films accuse them of that—but, in both films, characters are
actively searching for themselves and conducting important personal
journeys and having epiphanies that add up to them leaving the films
differently than they entered. They spend the films exploring inter-
nally, and trying on personas or comparing themselves to those around
them as a way of figuring out who they are. In *The Breakfast Club*,
they are tasked with writing an essay explaining who they are, and
complete the assignment in a way that is far more complex and honest than their principal originally imagined. Far from slackering, they
are doing tremendous amounts of important work figuring out who
they are. This is not just because they are teenagers in active identity-
formation mode, but because they are nearing college which, for them,
is like knowing an apocalypse is coming because it means their world
is ending.

In both films, college is the elephant in the room, a metaphor for the real world, a place they are afraid of, because they will be forced to leave the comfortable nest of high school and forced to move closer to becoming the adults they fear replicating. Contrast the intense self-exploration, dislocation from and fear of the real world in those John Hughes films with the portrayal of youth in another film, one that many have pointed out as a fascinating depiction of millenials: *Election*.

The 1999 film starred Reese Witherspoon as Tracy Flick, an obsessive, socially aggressive, hyperentitled overachiever who steadfastly believes that if she does everything right she will get everything she wants. Far from apathetic or dislocated from society, Flick is fighting to become student body president, which feels no less important to her than becoming the president of the United States. She spends little to no time gazing into her soul; it seems she feels she's perfect. She has no anxiety about her parents; Her mother is a helicopter mom and is still her best friend. Her main competitor for the presidency is Paul Metzler, an effortlessly popular athlete who coasts through life getting almost every break imaginable, never needing to explore himself, never dreaming of dropping out of society. Fear college? These two can't wait to go to college and see how much better the future will be. These characters would not only be aliens in the world of a John Hughes film, but we can imagine them watching the movies and struggling to understand why the characters in *Ferris Bueller's* and *The Breakfast Club* are so introspective and apathetic and afraid of college. (The other major candidate for office—the only true subversive teenage presence in the film—is Metzler's younger sister Tammy, who is portrayed as a serious clown and viewed by those in the film with fear or disdain. It's not long before she is suspended and placed in another school, signaling the central world of the movie has no place for someone so subversive.)

The disgruntled gen Xer in their midst is their ne'er-do-well teacher, Jim McAllister, played by Matthew Broderick. This is a deliciously ironic choice and surely not coincidental: Between *WarGames* and *Ferris Bueller's Day Off*, Broderick became emblematic of gen X on film. Casting him as the adult in *Election* is more resonant than casting almost any other actor would be. McAllister regards Flick's faith in herself and in the system with disgust and disdain. He seems symbolic of gen X looking down at the larger, peppier, more confident, better parented millenial gen and hating them. McAllister resents Flick so deeply that, when he sees her ecstatically celebrating because she thinks that she's going to be elected president, he does something shocking: He uses his power as the teacher in charge of the election to sabotage her victory by throwing away two crucial votes. Naturally, his deception is caught and reversed by an older janitor who's clearly a boomer. It's like generational warfare played out in miniature.

Many have noted that the films touted to be portraits of gen X rarely portray the Black experience or don't include Blacks within their discussion of gen X. In the world of John Hughes, it seems that Blacks don't exist. That's true, and a fair critique of Hughes's work. But the most iconic Black films of gen X's youth—*Do the Right Thing, Poetic Justice*, and *Menace II Society*—certainly traffic in characters who feel apathetic, dystopic, nihilistic, and dislocated from society. *Menace* and *Poetic Justice* are especially ripe with these feelings, as they're filled with teenage boys who are man-children, some because of broken nuclear families; they appear forgotten or abandoned or neglected by society. After years of living in an area filled with gangs, drugs, guns, and other Black men who kill each other wantonly, they have been shaped into people who are spiritually cut off from the rest of humanity. We see this most clearly when O-Dog, the breakout character in *Menace*, is needlessly insulted by a fearful Asian store owner. He responds to her offensive but impotent words by killing her, which shows how little he values human life—both hers and his. He's so disconnected from the importance of life that he thinks nothing of ending her life and risking a life sentence in prison over a remark. He then snatches the store's security camera videotape which he shows to his friends with pride. It's violence porn but it wouldn't be nearly as exciting if it weren't starring him, so it's a trophy of O-Dog's depravity. The character may or may not have heard of gen X but he is manifesting gen X values through the lens of South Central Los Angeles.

I have encountered some Black people who dispute the entire gen X meme, as if it somehow does not fit them but only fits whites. Dr. Dre famously said, "I haven't heard anyone in my hood talking about it. The only x I know is Malcolm X." [24] That's silly. Just because you and your friends don't sit around discussing meta ways of assessing the generation doesn't make it fake. And, yes, the media portrayals of gen X, from the movies to the news reports, have tended to focus exclusively on the white middle class. It's appropriate to critique the media vision of gen X as unfairly whitewashed, but to say that Blacks are not part of gen X is short-sighted. Can the Black community be said to have escaped the key touchstones that shaped gen X: divorce, latchkey kids, AIDS, crack, hiphop, MTV, and widespread economic troubles? No. Those things are absolutely part of the experience of Black people who grew up in the 1970s and 1980s. So, how can Blacks not be part of the gen X meme? Of course we are. Tupac and Snoop are just as good at expressing the gen X sense of dystopia and dislocation as Nirvana and REM. The gen X psychographic is larger than racial or class boundaries, even if the media portrayals are not. Sure, what it means to be in gen X operates differently in different neighborhoods but if the cultural touchstones that impact gen X also impact the Black community during gen X, then how are we not part of the story?

The concept of generation X is real. It's not a false grouping imposed from the top. We can argue about the name: Many in my generation hate the name and that's fair, it's not a great name, but we're stuck with it. However, some of that hate is wrapped up in hating the presence of a name and the attempt to explain who we are in a pithy way, so no matter what name we had it would be hated. Even if we had a different name, the touchstones would still be there and that's what shapes us. It's indisputable that there's a large group of Americans who are molded by the cultural, political, economic, and sociological things that happened in the 1970s and 1980s and the results of being the small, apathetic generation that followed a large, optimistic generation that attempted to revolutionize America. Denying that is futile. And gen X Americans have lived within a negative political climate our whole lives, causing widespread alienation, disaffection, and apathy. This, against a backdrop of events like the rise of a mysterious sexual plague and a powerful drug ruining society and harbingers of the end of American global dominance: All of that had the feel of the beginning of the end of days. So, it makes sense that the first Prince song to capture a giant audience and become his first monster hit was a song all about apathy and apocalypse.

The oldest gen Xers were in high school when Prince arrived on the national scene with his fifth album and a single that spoke of the funkiest armageddon scene you've ever heard of: *1999*. It was a perfect gen X dance song built on the idea that the world's about to end so, to hell with it, let's dance. It came out in 1982, two years into Ronald Reagan's first term, when the Cold War had reached a fever pitch and we seemed closer than ever to the brink of nuclear war. We had less faith in government and authority than any generation before us, which just deepened our sense that politics was meaningless fools' play. Who, in this climate, could respect authority? Surely, the people running the world were moronic if they were inching us to the brink of mutually assured destruction. In the face of that, the optimism of the 1960s seemed downright Pollyannaish. This was not something we could march to change. This was something from which we could do nothing but unplug. Given all that, "1999" fit perfectly.

In this song, the apocalypse has arrived—bombs are overhead, the sky is all purple, and people are running for their lives—our nuclear nightmares are fully realized. Then Prince and his bandmates sing, "Tried to run from my destruction. You know I didn't even care." What a seminal line for gen X. The end is near. What are we going to do? Dance. And shrug. And have an ecstatic party. Because we're smart enough to be apathetic; we know we can't change this. We can ask painful questions like, "Mommy? Why does everybody have the bomb?" But, instead of imbuing the song with a sense of hope or resistance, it's resigned to its fate. We never thought we had a chance anyway. "Life is just a party," Prince sings, "and parties weren't meant to last," so it figures that this would happen. "Everybody's got a bomb. Could all die any day." How cynical. There's not a slacker ethos at play: Prince proposes we do something, just something that has nothing to do with political protest. We should party. It's more of a spiritual protest that involves turning our back on politics. Society is falling apart, war is all around us, the leaders are power mad and myopic, war is imminent, the sky is turning ominous colors, and in Prince's world, in their last moments before the end, people are dancing. It's entropy, set to a funky beat.

Prince played with apocalyptic rhetoric in part because, in the early 1980s, the apocalypse truly seemed to be around the corner all the time. Whenever Prince cast his reporter's eye out his window he saw a world crumbling and about to end. "America" is the name of the fourth and last single from *Around the World in a Day* and, crucially, the first song on the album's second side. (It was released at a time when cassettes and vinyl still mattered, which meant sequencing was still important.) "America" gives us an entirely different vision of the world than the utopian one Prince laid out in the album's title song. The song is a sardonic reimagining of the patriotic classic "America the Beautiful," which opens with what sounds like the record itself struggling to get started, as if it were an old car or a lawn mower starting, dying, then starting again, which anticipates the world of troubles in America that's about to be described. Even the song itself isn't working properly and is having trouble getting going. Once the song launches, we get Prince's electric guitar playing "America the Beautiful" in lower, darker notes than the original. It signals the critique implicit in the song, because that old familiar melody is now dripping with irony, like a sonic version of the American flag repainted in black and white, the colors bleeding downward in a messy way. Where "1999" proposed an apathetic solution to the problem of the oncoming apocalypse—dance!—in "America" Prince sees dystopia and offers nothing but what he sees: No solutions, no boomerish optimism, he's just a camera. He sees an America in deep economic trouble, living in fear of communist Russia and fighting a losing battle against educational apathy and youthful drug abuse. There are aristocrats, America's upper class, climbing the corporate ladder, and there's a poor young woman dying in a one-room cage fit for a monkey, and then there's Jimmy Nothing. His name tells you how far he'll get in life. In the chorus, Prince sings, "Keep the children free," but it seems like that'll be hard to do in this world.

All this is not nearly as bleak as the world Prince paints two years later in the title song and first single from *Sign "O" The Times*. It's a bluesy plaint, a heart-rending portrait of a world dragged down by AIDS, gangs, crack, gun violence, the space-shuttle disaster and the overwhelmingly long shadow of nuclear war. Again, there are no solutions in sight. The chorus is just Prince simply saying "time," almost saying the world is in so bad a state that it's got him all but speechless. He concludes, a bit surprisingly, that he's still willing to fall in love, get married, and have a baby, so he's not totally nihilistic; he hasn't given up on life but he doesn't see anything to hope for. Yet, to an audience of gen Xers who see the world his way and are apathetic, disengaged, hopeless, and cynical, Prince's worldview fits and lets them know they can trust him. He knows what's goin' on.

Prince's relationship to gen X is influenced by his being a late boomer; a different breed than their older counterparts. Late boomers are aware of the dream of the 1960s but they are also shaped by the failures and death of that dream, by the way that the 1960s did not change the world completely and by the spirit-crushing disappointments of the 1970s. Just like gen X, they're shaped by the reasons why the optimism of the 1960s turns into the apathy and entropy of the 1980s.

Some call the last half of the baby boomers "Generation Jones" because its members were too young to have been shaped by the Utopianism of the 1960s, too young to have experienced Woodstock. Generation Jones members tend to be less optimistic and more cynical than boomers; they're trending toward the emotions that will mark gen X. This is another way Prince's space in the boomer gen prepares him to speak to gen X. But late boomers are still boomers which is why Prince's sound and look immediately recalls many boomer icons, and his music gave us some 1960s ideals. He looked and sounded like Hendrix or Santana standing in front of Sly's band, and danced in heeled boots in a James Brownish way, while playing music clearly inspired by Brown, Joni Mitchell, Curtis Mayfield, the Beatles, and the Stones. Prince has an unbridled and unironic love of the sixties, so when he goes to pay homage to the decade with *Around the World in a Day*, he summons the psychedelic era of the Beatles, especially *Sgt. Pepper's Lonely Hearts Club Band*, the zenith of the decade's ethos musically, the album that then and now stands for what the dream of the sixties was about.

Around the World in a Day's title track, the album's opening song, begins with a hypnotic, wailing sitar that recalls Indian music (and, for most mainstream American listeners, the Beatles' use of it), then flows into a psychedelic groove that reminds you of 1960s sounds. It's akin to announcing, "Here comes Prince's take on the sixties." The lyrics that follow confirm it. He begins, "Open your heart, open your mind," speaking to the sort of optimism and spiritual freedom and intellectual curiosity that marked the sixties. He's telling us of "a wonderful trip" on a train that's leaving any time for which the price is only laughter. This is very hippie territory. When we get to the chorus where the refrain is "No shouting," I feel like I'm in an ashram. The song ends with important but barely audible words, which in itself recalls the hidden messages of those late Beatles albums. Prince says, "A government of love and music boundless in its unifying power, a nation of alms, the production, sharing of ideas, a shower of flowers." This is rose-tinted utopianism. This is unity, love, and LSD. It's relevant that he ends on the word flower because the image of the flower child, the peace-sign–sprouting woman with daisies in her hair, remains one of the enduring symbols of the dream of the sixties. When boomers heard *Around the World in a Day* they may have felt it to be like sonic comfort food, a lovingly nostalgic recreation of their era's sounds and its ethos.

But he wasn't a boomer star. He was the perfect age to be a wise and cool big brother to gen X. Prince may be a generational hybrid, able to speak to both boomers and gen Xers (and, now, millenials), but he's a special icon for my generation. When we think of the 1980s and 1990s, we usually think of Nirvana or Tupac or REM, but Prince's surreal run of albums from 1982's *1999* to 1992's *Symbol*, and the messages in his music that speak to the particular gen X zeitgeist make him a central figure for that generation.

One of the most important issues in the conversation between

Prince and gen X was sex. Gen X was more sexually aware and more sexually active at an earlier age than any other generation and, at the same time, we were fraught with anxiety because of the frighteningly rapid spread of the deadliest sexually transmitted disease in human history. Overlay those two developments with Prince's intense sexuality, which is lustful and sensual and so knowing it seems like the product of more experience than anyone but a king with a harem could ever hope to have, and you can see why gen X was filled with people who were hungry to hear what Prince had to say.

2

The King of Porn Chic

THE VIDEOCASSETTE RECORDER, the now defunct but once seminal device better known as the VCR, was invented in 1952, but didn't become popular until the late 1970s, when the device was perfected by European and Japanese companies and, also, not coincidentally, when low-cost videotapes became widely available featuring pornography. It's like a lightbulb went off in the minds of corporations and consumers: This device made it possible for people to watch porn in the privacy of their own homes and on their own schedule. Never before had so many people had such easy, private access to so much porn. A wave hit: Hundreds of thousands of VCRs were sold to early adopters, enabling or motivating producers to lower the price, leading to millions being sold. Soon enough, most American homes had a VCR and, with it, the possibility of surreptitiously watching porn.

This technology opened up the experience for many people, including gen X teenagers, and led to the destigmatization of porn, a change that reverberated throughout the mainstream. Watching it no longer automatically meant you were a pervert: Too many were watching to stigmatize them all. This was a change from the sexual climate of the sixties where free love and the pill and the condom and *Playboy* magazine had sexually liberated America and sex was an expression of freedom and joy. The eighties normalization of porn, and its harder, rougher, loveless vision of sex, made America wilder, at least in the media. The ubiquity of porn sped up the sexualization of American imagery that had begun before the VHS boom. Sped it up like the Millennium Falcon going into light speed. Eventually, a full menu of soft-core porn was available via cable, which rocketed in popularity through the 1980s.

Mainstream movies responded by depicting wilder or more graphic sex scenes. You see the entrance of the porn aesthetic, or porn chic, in popular early eighties films like *Risky Business, Flashdance, American Gigolo, Angel Heart, Bolero, Nine ½ Weeks,* and others. Even the 1983 film from the Star Wars franchise nodded to the times, with the unforgettable image of Princess Leia in a copper bikini, reduced to being a sexual slave laying beside the tail of Jabba the Hut, who kept her close with a chain and collar. This is unmistakable S&M imagery, which typically shows submissives kneeling pliantly and obediently at the feet of dominants who often hold onto them via a chain. Leia as a humiliated submissive in Jabba's dominant fantasy is one of the most blatant examples of BDSM (bondage, dominance, discipline, submission, sadism, and masochism) slipping into mainstream popular culture.

Prince played right into that vibe and perhaps contributed to it with his highly sexual and quasiautobiographical 1984 movie *Purple Rain*, which fit in a world where the slew of pornographic magazines in the marketplace swelled and the imagery in mainstream magazines like *Esquire, Rolling Stone*, and *Sports Illustrated* grew more overtly sexualized. Pauline Kael wrote about *Purple Rain* in *The New Yorker:* "He [Prince] knows how he wants to appear—like Dionysus crossed with a convent girl on her first bender." [1]

There's a pornish aesthetic to the entire film. It's like a porno set in the world of a nightclub. There's little actual sex but lots of innuendo and steaminess; much of the movie feels like a prelude to sex scenes. Prince and Apollonia ride to a lake on his motorcycle and she jumps into what she thinks is Lake Minnetonka: The scene could be easily inserted into a porno as a buildup to boning. Later, we see them having sex in a barn, which is something often see in porn or *Playboy*. There's an amateurish, faux-natural quality to much of the acting and direction that recalls porn. And there's lots of boldly sexual imagery: Apollonia performs in lingerie, Wendy gets on her knees and simulates giving Prince head as he plays guitar during "Computer Blue," Prince shows you his sex stroke during "Darling Nikki" and, at the film's end, he shoots water from the end of his guitar as he strokes the neck of his axe, which makes it look like he's masturbating and coming all over the crowd. *Purple Rain* almost was rated X because of the sex scene between Prince and Apollonia, though there seem to be several other scenes that may have contributed to that narrowly avoided X.

All of Prince's performances are hypersexual; he does "Computer Blue" with no shirt on. Morris Day's performances are hypersexual, too. He blithely and caricaturishly embraces stereotypes about the animalistic nature of Black sex by doing his hit "Jungle Love," where we hear whoops from some sort of simian in heat, and see him wearing an animal-print–collared blazer. It's also fascinating to watch the male vanity parade that is Prince and Morris, both of whom are so sexual and so fixated on their appearance that they're obsessively fastidious, constantly checking themselves out in a mirror or fixing their hair or at least looking like they've spent lots of time putting themselves together. Few films give us two Black men of such outsized sexuality and vanity, always looking like they're about to get someone in bed. The only one that comes to mind is Spike Lee's *Mo' Better Blues*, starring Denzel Washington and Wesley Snipes. As musicians.

Another way that *Purple Rain* answered the Zeitgeist of the 1980s is in the way it spoke to the power of MTV, which Prince recognized quickly. All of gen X's central dynamics came together in MTV, which at the time was the most influential media institution of them all. Back in the 1980s, MTV shaped the taste of its era by directing us toward more visual artists. Early in MTV's life, Prince saw that it would revolutionize music and lead people to interact with music differently. Thus he leapt to capitalize not just with videos, but also with what was essentially a movie-length video. Prince began shooting his first film the year MTV was launched. Less than two years after MTV was launched, he was working on *Purple Rain*. Alan Leeds said the need for visuals came to shape Prince's mind-set. "One day we were in the studio and he was playing me something and then he told me the video vision he had for the song. I looked at him and said, 'You just wrote this song this morning and cut this song today and you already have a video in mind?' He said, 'Alan, what you don't understand is people don't hear music anymore, they see music.' He knew that MTV had radically changed how people absorb new music and this was a medium he could use to become who he wanted to be. That's what *Purple Rain* was."

It's meaningful, and very gen X of him, that Prince repeatedly aided his career by being open to technological advances. Long before he had showed his early understanding of the value of MTV, he was an early adopter of the Linn LM-1 drum machine, which used digital samples of acoustic drums. It allowed him to get great sounding drums quickly and with minimal assistance, and it launches his most productive period. Years later, when he was slipping from the elite ranks, and the Internet was young (and called the World Wide Web or the information superhighway), Prince was active online and a pioneer in using the net to communicate with fans. "Before he changed his name to an unpronounceable symbol there was a newsgroup called alt.music .prince, starting in '93, on Prodigy and Compuserv and then AOL," said Anil Dash, a blogger, Internet entrepreneur, and technologist. "These are among the first live synchronous gatherings of fans online. The Prince fan base did Paisley Park chats on Sunday nights but then he started showing up, laying the groundwork for what would today be a social media campaign."

Prince also built a website called www.thedawn.com in 1996, released an authorized song through the original Napster, and distributed his music directly to fans long before anyone else did. "That's authentically using the tech," Dash told me. "He's completely fluent in it. He's knowing how the tech works and using it to amplify himself. That's loving the machines, that's loving the tech, and I think there's a very intrinsic gen X thing of the computers are ours to use. Computers had not been microcomputers until the eighties and the radical change of having a personal computer was you own it, you control it, you program it. It's gen Xish to take control of the computers. It's the gen X birthright to see technology as something you'll control as opposed to something you'll ask permission to use. Take these tools and bend them to your will and it's disruptive to society, and to industries and to culture. I'll take these things and make them mine and that's all over the gen X moment."

Millions of gen X teenagers were latchkey kids or kids with relatively large amounts of free time to watch racy movies or soap operas or smoke weed or drink alcohol or have sex or read sex advice literature like *The Joy of Sex*, which came out in 1972 and remained wildly popular for years. During the 1980s, a tiny, old, matronly woman who didn't strike anyone as sexual became a national icon for her cheerfully frank discussions of sexuality. I'm talking about Dr. Ruth Westheimer. She was just another part of the normalization of sexuality going on throughout the era. We also had boldly sexual music, like disco, rock, soul, punk, New Jack Swing, Madonna, and Prince.

Many gen X teens also, crucially, had their own telephones. In the 1980s it became common for middle-class teenagers to have a phone they could use in a private space—either their own line or a phone in their room or a superlong cord—all of which facilitated having conversations the adults couldn't hear, conversations that were often about sex, either talking to a potential partner or strategizing with friends about potential partners. Gen Xers also had more private TV access, either watching the family's communal set alone or having a set in their room. In gen X, TV becomes less of a shrine that gathers the family and more of a boob tube, offering sex and sedation to an audience of singular, zoned-out viewers. All the free time, the altered cultural climate, and the technological changes gave gen X both freedom and stimulation and led to more teenagers having more sex and at an earlier age than ever before in history.

One study found that among women who were eighteen in 1988, 70 percent said they had had sex, a leap from 1980, when that number was 56 percent, and from 1970 when it was just 40 percent. The proportion of fifteen-year-olds who were sexually active also jolted upward, the percentage of teenage girls who used some method of contraception the first time they had sex leapt as well, demonstrating that not only were kids having sex but they were also getting sexual education and implementing it.

Meanwhile, a horrifying sexual cancer was growing. It wouldn't be detected until the mid-1980s. A plague was spreading that would kill many millions and change the way the world viewed sex forever. In the mid-1980s, when we began talking about AIDS, it was rising at a frightening rate, and doctors didn't understand how it was happening. People were afraid that they would get it if they kissed someone or hugged someone or sat on the wrong toilet seat. It was a microscopic monster that could mysteriously kill anyone, quickly. We heard about people getting AIDS the first time they had sex; so, it wasn't punishment for promiscuity, it was Russian roulette. People didn't stop having sex, but there was widespread fear and anxiety and the decision to have a new partner or a regular partner you couldn't trust 100 percent became fraught with the potential of death.

Into a world influenced by these changed circumstances—the prevalence of teen sex, the mainstreaming of porn chic in popular culture, and a rising fear of sexual contact itself—came Prince, the most sexual musician popular music had seen in decades. Perhaps ever. Dickerson said Prince made a conscious decision to be known that way. "There was a point where we were in LA early on," Dickerson said, "and we were in a break between shows and he sat everybody down and said, 'Okay, here's what we're going to do. Everybody in this band is going to have a distinct personality and identity. I'm going to portray pure sex.' Those were his exact words. And everybody else had to get a handle on what they were going to be. So, that was declared from that point forward. Pure sex meant taking the piss out of every taboo and shocking people in every way he could come up with. He was kind of like a precocious kid who's doing things to get a rise out of the adults. He had a lot of that in him but in a very calculated, very wise beyond his years way. And, looking back, now that I'm a strategist and brand marketer, he was pure genius. It's a time-honored technique in the entertainment business to create a persona and then create a sense of wonder in the minds of people who have to wonder whether or not this guy is really from another planet, an otherworldly being. And that was just an instinct that marketing genius he had innately."

Dickerson explained that it's Prince's marketing genius and his desire to shock and play with taboos that led him to tease people into thinking he could be gay. "He was courting controversy as a business tactic," Dickerson said. "As a marketing tactic. So Prince didn't back away from suggestions of homosexuality. It was almost like a martial arts move where you use your opponent's momentum against him. I still get the question to this day: Is Prince gay? What? This is the most drivenly heterosexual man I've ever known. But he was intrigued by using all of it. People like Bowie had used that as a branding tool and Prince seized on that and used it as well as anybody." Erykah Badu once told me that to succeed as a pop star fans have got to want to be you or to have sex with you. Prince satisfied both conditions.

In his work in the early 1980s, Prince was playing with gender norms, shocking people with the audacity of his androgyny in a time when many musicians were toying with it. He was wearing heels and eyeliner and earrings and thongs and stockings and blouses that were wide open to the navel, showing his curly, masculine chest hair, practically cross-dressing in public while singing in a falsetto. He pushed that envelope both sartorially and lyrically. Prince asked, in the song "Controversy," "Am I straight or gay?" and didn't answer. He did answer elsewhere on that album, on a song called "Uptown," a story song where a woman asks him "Are you gay?" He says, "No. Are you?" If sexuality can be plotted as a continuum, Prince was dancing in the middle, alongside Michael Jackson, while most other men in pop music were on the edges, leaving little doubt who they were going home with. On one side there was Boy George, Morrissey, Depeche Mode, Erasure, The Pet Shop Boys, George Michael, and others. At the other end of the continuum was Guns N' Roses, Run-DMC, U2, LL Cool J—sexual alphas so hyper-macho it seemed certain there wasn't a shred of anima inside them.

Anima is psychologist Carl Jung's term for the feminine part of a man's personality, as opposed to *animus*, the masculine part of a woman's personality. Machismo can be thrilling to women but a fully integrated man who embraces his female side and thus understands women on a deep level can also be thrilling. Prince maximized his sexual potential by wearing his anima on his sleeve. It was as if Prince's connection with his anima was evidence of the depth of his relationships with women and proof that he was an expert on women because he was so in touch with the woman inside him. Was it just about getting attention and shocking people as Dickerson said, or was there something deeper? Well, just as Prince used his band to attempt to fulfill his familial needs, some think that perhaps his self-feminization sprung somehow from overcompensating for the void caused by lack of a relationship with his mother.

Prince's overactive anima came to life most vividly in "If I Was Your Girlfriend," written when he was breaking up with Susannah Melvoin. In the song, he imagines himself as female and in a platonic relationship with a woman that's more intimate than it could be if he were her male lover. But, toward the end of the song, he returns to a male voice, still trying to get to the intimacy that female best friends share. He's begging not for sex, but for the closeness that women know can be more powerful than sex. Interesting to see someone who runs from intimacy in his real life expressing his desire for it so strongly here; perhaps this is indicative of someone who wants intimacy but is also scared of it. He wants to bond and nurture the way close female friends do: brush her hair, go to the movies and cry together. Where so many men are callous or insensitive, he clearly values her feelings. He sings, in one of the deepest lyrics in all of his oeuvre, "Would you run to me if somebody hurt you, even if that somebody was me?" Could I be the shoulder you cry on and could the bond between us be so deep that I'm the one you want holding you after I made you cry? Could I be your salvation if I'm the sinner? When he snaps back to a male perspective he remains female focused, sweetly trying to win her over in a way that he thinks she would want, ways that move through intimacy rather than traditional masculine expressions of sexuality. He offers a tickle war that'll make her laugh and laugh then suggests he'll kiss her down there where it counts and "drink every ounce" and then they'll have the ultimate cuddlefest: "I'll hold u tight and hold u long and together we'll stare into silence and we'll try 2 imagine what it looks like." People say Prince did crave that sort of intimacy in his relationships with women even as he struggled with the intimacy he wanted.

Two lines in "If I Was Your Girlfriend" stand out after talking with people close to Prince. When he's imagining himself as her girlfriend he sings, "Would u let me wash your hair?" And later as a man he says, "Would u let me give u a bath?" Those desires I'm told are part of his real life. Someone who was intimate with him and knows others who were, too, says Prince was not doing exactly as much screwing as he'd have you believe. I was told by someone who knows that Prince loves to bathe women. And brush their hair. And sometimes he did these things in lieu of intercourse. It was not part of trying to get laid or deepen the sexual experience, but as a worshipful appreciation of femininity. A person who was close to Prince said, "One girl told me that she got frustrated because he'd rather bathe her."

A woman who was in a relationship with Prince years ago told me that when he gave women baths he took total control. "He ran the bath, he put the bubbles in, he took your clothes off, he washed you, he washed your hair, it was a whole procedure and process. He put lotion on you after. He'd give you a robe. I don't know if it was worshipful or if it was sweet and sensitive." She said sex with Prince was, well, many things. "It was always intimidating for me. Because it was Prince. I never lost sight of that it was Prince. He was never a normal dude. He's creative, yes, but he's not as wild as everyone thinks, though I've heard he has a propensity to be. The act of it with me was not as freaky, not as wild as you might expect, it wasn't 'Dirty Mind,' 'Erotic City,' but I know from other girls that I've talked to that it has been. The room looked like it would've been with the props how you'd imagine but the actual act itself was kind of romantic. More loving than freaky. He never made you feel gross or cheap or that you were one of many. I never felt unimportant. He always made you feel beautiful and perfect. He was very soft, he was like a coach. I would do something to him and he would show me the way he wanted it done if it wasn't the way he wanted it. He's very gentle. Very gentle. And thoughtful. He was the most patient man I've been with. And the most complicated in terms of being in bed with. The most sensitive, the most androgynous, the most balance of male/female energy. He was the closest thing that I'd had to having a woman. It wasn't like having sex with a man. It was bigger than that. It was erotic and unique." In many ways her interactions with Prince reminded her of relating to a woman. "He's in touch with things most guys don't pick up on, small things or details. They just don't, but he reminds me of a woman or of being in a relationship with a woman in that every subtle action you do is noticed without having to be explained. He gets the way you gesture or the way your eyes move down or he can sense insecurity. He's also very masculine but not in a dude way, in a man way, like, strong. He's confident but he's as impatient as he is patient. He's both things at the same time. He's a true Gemini. He's masculine but he's in touch with his femi-

ninity. It's complicated." She told me that even "during sex he's still
performing, his expressions are overt and thought out and not natural.
You'd go over and he'd be composed and dressed to the nines and his
actions are intentional. Even when he's light and easy he's being controlled." She said he loved to be with multiple girls, or to watch. "He
had threesomes and he liked that quite a bit. He had girls have sex in
front of him and he liked that quite a bit. He was into girls having
experiences with each other around him. He would send a girl over to
talk to me while he was watching from upstairs, to watch the interaction. Or he'd say, 'She has a beautiful body doesn't she?'"

White America has long viewed Black sexuality with fear and fasci-
nation, certain that Blacks are better endowed and more sexual and
having more sex and having it with more abandon. This is not a comment on Black biology or the Black cultural approach to sex, but a
comment on white America's perception of those things. In *Nobody
Knows My Name*, James Baldwin famously wrote, "To be an American
Negro male is to be a kind of walking phallic symbol: which means
that one pays, in one's own personality, for the sexual insecurity of
others." During slavery, the image of the uncontrollable, animalistic
Black buck who wanted to defile the pristine white woman was used
to keep America afraid of and in control of Black people. The imagery
remains, if only in the collective subconscious.

   "Black male sexuality is always going to be a threat in America,"
Questlove said. "And Prince came along at the right time. America still
had post-*Mandingo* dreams, no matter how it looked. Which really
weren't getting met by Michael Jackson. I remember a lot of inter-

views when Prince started catching on where they asked people, 'Why do you like Prince?' and they said, 'Well, Michael Jackson's cool, but Prince gives us more sex.' He knows you draw more bees with honey than with vinegar."

White America's love of Black popular culture has often been wrapped up in its electric attraction to Black sexuality. But rarely has Black sexuality been presented in such a raw, rough, wild, carnally dangerous, bigendered form as it was in the body and persona of Prince. You knew for certain that a woman alone with him would get turned out. However, in most of his music the opposite was happening: Prince worships women so much that in his songs he usually gets turned out by them. His stories were less about "This is what I'll do to you," than "This is what I want you to do to me." That had a way of empowering the women he was speaking about, giving them agency and sexual force, rather than making bodies or conquests. His sexual narratives are rarely about being dominant—they don't posit Prince as an undeniably seductive Casanova. Prince's pen gave us women as aggressors who pick him up and/or are more sexual and promiscuous than him. One example: "Darling Nikki."

No Prince song more clearly articulates porn chic coming to life in mainstream culture than "Darling Nikki." The song seems like a porno distilled into a song. The ominous, steamy rock vamp at the outset builds into a wildly kinky vibe, then the lyrics really take you there. This is a story song like few others. Our sex god tells us he met a woman who's far wilder than he—the first thing we learn about her is she was a sex fiend he met while she was masturbating in a hotel lobby. What an image. Not only can I picture her, but I feel she's not a whore who'll grab any man, but a sexually voracious lover who picks Prince because she sees something in his strut or his outfit that suggests he just might be ready for her level of sexuality. Crucially: He does not pick her up. She picks him up saying, "How'd you like to waste some time?" From the beginning of their interaction she's in control and she remains so when they're at her castle where wild, passionate, mind-blowing sex happens instantly, just as in a porno. He can't tell you what she did to him, but his body will never be the same. She's turning him out! He screams, "Her lovin' will kick your behind! Oh, she'll show you no mercy!" Unlike many other sexual men in music, Prince is a sexual alpha who's unafraid to tell stories about women who flipped his wig. Such is his comfort with his sexual power. And when he wakes up the next morning, she's gone. She did the "Wham-bam-thank-you-man" thang to him!

"Little Red Corvette" is another masterfully written pornish sex story song, in which Prince quickly has wild sex with an intimidatingly experienced woman who puts a certain fear in him that he must overcome. In this song, it's as though Prince is a sexual athlete whose competition is women who are more sexual than he is. He feels pressure in the form of performance anxiety but pushes through it to have explosive intercourse. Great writing gives important characters memorable entrances and like Nikki, the woman in "Little Red Corvette" gets a great entrance: The way she parks her car sideways lets him know it's not going to last. Somehow, from her parking style, he discerns that she's a man-eater. This is confirmed a moment later in one of the great lines in pop songwriting history: "She had a pocketful of horses / Trojans and some of them used." It's titillating, funny, and gross. Prince fully realizes the sexual monster he's dealing with after she drives him home: "I felt a little ill, when I saw all the pictures, of the jockeys that were there before me. Believe it or not, I started to worry. Wondered if I had enough class." Of course, he does find it in him to be the sexual champion he expects of himself. We know this when he says, "Girl, you got an ass like I never seen! And the ride! I say, the ride is so smooth! You must be a limousine!" Confirmation of his sexual success is not fully discernable from the lyrics but is made clear by the way he sings, "You must be a limousine" with a transcendent scream that suggests being in orgasmic ecstasy.

Over and again in Prince's sexual songs the woman is the more powerful sexual agent: not just Nikki and the girl with the Red Corvette but also Camille, as described in "Shockadelica," where, as soon as the lights go out, "The smell of doom, is creepin into your lonely room. The bed's on fire. Your fate is sealed. And you're so tired. And the reason is Camille." The chorus says, "The girl must be a witch. She got your mind, body, and soul hitched." Later: "She'll make you beg . . . Got you in a trance. Cuz when this woman say dance, you dance!" The man who worships women is repeatedly dominated by them. (He told you in "Kiss," "Women, not girls, rule my world.") And once again, she's not just figuratively in the driver's seat, but literally as well. He sings, "When you've cried enough, maybe she'll let you up, for a nasty ride in her shockadeli-car." Prince consistently places the woman in the driver's seat as a symbol of her sexual power and a way of saying she's in charge. In "Little Red Corvette," she drives him to the place where her horses run free. In "Darling Nikki," he says, "She took me to her castle." And, in "Lady Cab Driver," he's in the back of her cab. That song, too, is like a porno in that after a bit of dialogue—we learn he's sad and lonely and asks if he can pay the fare via his tears—poof, they're suddenly screwing. We flash-cut from Prince in the cab sharing his feelings to doing it.

"Raspberry Beret" is another great pornish story song. Prince is a virgin who quickly and easily picks up a girl who walks into a store, in which, in great writing, he describes himself as a lazy employee: "It seems that I was busy doin' something close to nothing, but different than the day before." This may be read as a metaphor for his sexuality because, since he's a virgin, he's doing something close to nothing. Which reminds me a little of that classic moment from *The Breakfast Club* when Anthony Michael Hall's Brian finally confesses that he's a virgin and defends his not telling them sooner by saying, "Because it's my business. My personal business." To which Judd Nelson's Bender replies, "Well, Brian, it doesn't sound like you're doing any business." But I digress. In "Raspberry Beret" Prince shows off his short story writing talent by dashing off another great character entrance: The girl with the raspberry headwear shows who she is by walking in through the out door.

Prince puts the girl in the colorful chapeau on the back of his motorcycle, thus breaking his usual pattern where the woman dominating him is symbolized by her controlling the vehicle in which they ride. But, as usual, this woman is more sexually experienced than Prince. He sings, "I could tell when she kissed me, she knew how to get her kicks." She kisses him, meaning she's in charge, and she shows her experience through knowing how to enjoy sexuality. Curiously, Prince says she's not too bright, which is a weird outlier moment: He almost never insults women in his songs, in fact, he often looks up to them in some way, and he has nothing else negative to say about this woman so I'm not sure why he felt it necessary to describe her as kind of dumb. Anyway, they go someplace that is a classic porn milieu: "Down by old man Johnson's farm." Prince is obviously playing off *Johnson*, a slang term for penis, but there's so much more going on: She's riding on his motorcycle, a phallic symbol, to the place owned by Mr. Johnson, synonym for a phallic symbol, and then going into a barn, which can be read as a yonic symbol; well, that's a parade of sexual entendres.

He sets up the moment of coitus in writerly fashion: "The rain sounds so cool, when it hits the barn roof and the horses wonder who U are. Thunder drowns out what the lightning sees. Honey, U feel like a movie star." In that moment you would definitely feel like a certain kind of movie star: a porn star! The whole natural world is watching— the rain is falling, the horses are overhearing and saying, hey, who's that, the lightning is jolting down to see what they're doing. What an amazing anthropomorphic image—lightning that's watching humans do their thing like an electrified peeping Tom.

Once again, we get Prince treating a sexual encounter like a pressurized sports moment: When he finally confesses that it's his first time he concedes that most know not to expect much. Who would think Prince would deliver on an experienced hottie when it's his first time at the plate? Prince. And he does—he steps up because when Prince is alone with a beautiful woman he just knows how to please her in spite of his total lack of experience. "If I had the chance to do it all again, oh, I wouldn't change a stroke, cuz baby I'm the most, when a girl as fine as she walks in!" He delivers like a big-time athlete who always makes it happen in crunch time even though he's a rookie in his first game.

Many of the same themes come to play in "The Ballad of Dorothy Parker," a weird little story-song that gives us Prince with a woman with a quicker wit than his, which is what he says he was looking for. Once again a woman picks him up, seduces him, and emotionally dominates him. As usual they get to a sexual moment with porn-movie speed, though they don't consummate it, because his mind is on another woman. Dorothy wins him over by repeatedly affirming Prince's masculinity, saying, "Sounds like a real man to me," in response to him doing things that are more typically feminine, like ordering a fruit cocktail and insisting on keeping his pants on when they get into a bath together because he's "kinda goin' with someone," even though it's a relationship that he knows is on the rocks. This surely makes him feel comfortable and touches on the message: "Let people be whoever they want to be," that he explored in "Uptown."

Prince's obsession with bathing with women comes out here: Dorothy invites him to take a bath. Boy, did she hit the right note with that invitation. After he leaves her bath, he takes one with the lover he'd been fighting with, which solves everything. He sings, "I took another bubble bath with my pants on, all the fighting stopped, next time I'll do it sooner." Thus, we have bathing as a panacea or even a means to redemption or perhaps a sort of rebirth—of him or of the relationship—as part of change after immersion in water, also known as *baptism.*

Prince uses water as a symbol for cleansing, redemption, and baptism in many songs, including "Purple Rain" and "17 Days" where his response to his broken heart is, "Let the rain come down, let the rain come down." There's also the unforgettable and mysterious opening of "Computer Blue," when Lisa asks Wendy, "Is the water warm enough?" and, "Shall we begin?" Begin what? Wendy told Questlove she thought it referred to baptism. We also see Prince talking about bathing in "When 2 R In Love." The chorus: "Drop, drop, drop, drop. Water, water, water. Come bathe with me. Let's drown each other in each other's emotions. Bathe with me. Let's cover each other with perfume and lotion." Sounds like a real man to me.

When it comes to incredibly well-written songs about sex, nothing compares to "International Lover." In this one, Prince is fully in control of the sexual experience and is the one in the driver's seat—he's the pilot to her passenger in a song-long metaphor linking sex and flight that turns the plane crew's mundane instructions into comic but deadly sexual innuendos. "If 4 any reason there is a loss in cabin pressure, I will automatically drop down 2 apply more." And: "We are now making our final approach to satisfaction. Please bring your lips, your arms, your hips into the upped and locked position." My favorite lyric is: "In the event there is overexcitement, your seat cushion may be used as a flotation device." Rarely, if ever, had the mainstream heard songs describing sex in such lascivious detail, having fun with talking about sex by discussing it in poetic slow motion. You need only to listen to "International Lover" once to learn something about how to have sex.

The most shocking and telling of all Prince's sex story songs is the penultimate song on *Dirty Mind*, a ninety-one-second burst of minimalist funk about incest called "Sister." "That," Dickerson said, "was his volley in trying to push that sexual envelope further than it ever had been pushed."

Prince has three older half-sisters and it's known that he lived in Manhattan with one of them, Sharon, while he was a teenager searching for a record deal. Sharon is sixteen years older than Prince. In the song, he says he was sixteen and his sister was thirty-two. Friends told me he was closer to Sharon than his other siblings. No one knows if this story of incest is real or not. If it's not, it's evidence of Prince's lurid imagination and the way he performs identity and constructs himself to appear more lewd and screwed up than he actually is. But, if it is a true story, then, well, that's messed up. Either way, we begin to see why Prince became the sexual being he is.

The lyric that makes this one of the most important songs in the Prince canon, and far more than just an exercise in shock value, is this: "She's the reason for my, uh, sexuality." He's saying this story is key to understanding Prince, whether it's true or not, he wants it to be a central part of his past, or part of the mythology that he's creating, and thus a seminal part of what he wants you to think about him. But is it true? In 1983 Prince told *Rock & Soul* magazine, "Sister is pretty self-explanatory. It's not pro-incest and it's not a negative song about incest. It's just an experience. It should not be taken any other way than that. It's just an incident in my life. It's real, it's a subject that a lot of people try to avoid. I wish a lot of artists would try to write about reality instead of these big poetic visions that don't exist." Prince also told Bill Adler, then of *Rolling Stone*, that "Sister" was autobiographical. "Everything about my music is."[2]

The song and story should be read as crucial whether this incident happened or not, that is, whether he's talking about the real Prince (making the song into memoir) or talking about the imagined Prince (making the song into myth building). Either way, he wants you to think about this incident when you think about him. Whether it actually happened, he presents this moment of incest as epiphanic and thus it becomes part of his story: Early on he had a wild but loving but scary sexual experience with a sister he liked and that shaped him into the sexual creature we've come to know. For Prince, "Sister" is like the creation myth for a superhero: My hypersexual older sister seduced me and taught me all about wild sex as she made love to me and dominated me and all of that turned me into what I am today.

In "Sister," once again, Prince is the passive receiver of sex, the one who gets turned out by a woman far more experienced and powerful than he. He sets this up immediately by announcing she's double his age, lovely and loose. The way he says "loose" is crucial: He pauses before and after it so the word sort of hangs in the air all alone, isolating it, giving it emphasis, telling us he has no chance against her. He also tells us she doesn't wear underwear because she feels it stops her sexual juices from flowing. There's no doubt this puppy is going to get devoured. "She only wanted to turn me out," he says. But, curiously, he also says, "My sister never made love to anyone else but me," which is a heavy lyric I can't shake. Or totally understand. Does he mean she had sex with others but only with him did the connection rise to the level of lovemaking? So, she devours him, but tenderly, giving us not just incest and statutory rape but also, somehow, love? Really? He says, "Incest is everything it's said to be," which curiously affirms any thought imaginable about what incest could be. Destructive? Amazing? Painful? Transformative? Epiphanic? Yes, Prince says, and more. So Prince's sister shows him the sexual ropes, as in what a blow job is and where his dick is supposed to go, meaning she deflowered him. And he says, "She took a whip to me until I shout," which I take literally, as in, she introduced him to S&M. (Quite a lot of sexual education from your initial lover!) And at the song's end she maintains control over him—he sings, sounding desperate and frightened and frazzled, "Don't put me on the street again!" What does that mean? Don't put me out of your house? Or don't pimp me out? If this story gives us the reason for his sexuality then maybe Prince's worshipful stance toward women and his desire for warm, intimate, affirming relationships are a response to the harsh brand of love he experiences in his first relationship. I guess there could be love and tenderness in their weird coupling but it sure doesn't sound like it. And does it mean anything that, according to many who know her, Sharon is gay?

Questlove, who's analyzed the song closely, told me, "At the end there's this screaming, this anger. That's when I'm like, whoa. I just feel sorry for the narrator. You were naïve in the beginning and now you're screaming at the top of your lungs. And it's done in such a frantic, breathless pace." "Sister" not only ties Prince to the hypersexuality and porn chic of the gen X era but is also a metaphor for what arises in a broken family when, in the midst of the shattering, love becomes confusing and painful.

Gen X is also marked by growing up in a society that's more integrated than any in American history up to that point. It's no surprise that diversity, multiculturalism, political correctness, and affirmative action became buzzwords in the late seventies and eighties. We are the children of people who watched or participated in the battle to desegregate America and many of them taught us in word and deed to not be prejudiced, and that anything was possible for Black Americans. This is obviously not to suggest that racism ended or abated. The eighties gave us a new parade of people who became racialized memes, symbols of America's continuing tragic difficulties with race, from Willie Horton to Yusuf Hawkins to Edmund Perry to Bernard Goetz to the young men convicted and later exonerated for attacking the Central Park jogger—people who were victims or villains depending on who was looking, Rorschachs who divided America, story by story and perpetuated centuries-old troubles.

Meanwhile, gen Xers grew up in a world that also fed them evidence of a growing equality: a preponderance of Black leaders and stars they embraced or dreamt of being like and who contributed to the narrative of a new sort of Black empowerment. Suddenly, Black crossover appeal was more available and less stigmatized than ever before: In previous generations, crossing over equaled selling out, but not to gen Xers. This historical shift led to a slew of iconic Blacks who were idolized by both whites and Blacks. Michael Jackson became the world's biggest recording artist. Whitney Houston became one of the world's biggest recording artists. Eddie Murphy became the biggest star in Hollywood. Bill Cosby had the best-rated show on television. Michael Jordan became the biggest star in the sports world. Reverend Jesse Jackson ran for president twice. Oprah began constructing a TV empire. Spike Lee became a major Hollywood filmmaker. And Prince became a megastar. It's like they were the grownup children of the Motown aesthetic that preached embracing and accentuating your crossover potential. (The children of the Stax aesthetic of crossover free, nitty gritty hyper-Blackness were hanging out in what was then called *rap*, which was uncompromisingly Black and uninterested in crossover except on its own terms.)

Hanging over all this was Dr. Martin Luther King, Jr., whose shadow loomed over the 1980s as the ultimate example of a Black American who whites and Blacks both could and should idolize (as opposed to Malcolm X, Huey Newton, and Minister Louis Farrakhan, who were idolized by many Blacks and had no crossover appeal). In 1986, as gen X was growing up, the King holiday finally began being recognized. A few years later, just one month into the new decade, we saw the birth of what seemed like a new King, when Nelson Mandela was released from prison after twenty-seven years to reveal himself as yet another a towering global symbol of the power of peaceful resistance to racism and what can be achieved by a man who refuses to let racism turn him angry and bitter.

Gen X responded to these shifts with a new cultural biraciality: White kids became knowledgeable about Black culture and Black kids grew more knowledgeable about and open to white culture than ever before. Xers looked at cultural products made by other races as part of their own cultural legacy, ending any sense of a de facto segregation distancing these cultures. When *The Big Chill* came out in 1983, showing whites loving Motown music, some Blacks were shocked to realize that white late boomers felt Motown was part of their cultural legacy. No one would ever make that mistake about hiphop. We know whites feel hiphop belongs to them, too.

One of the products of this new cultural biraciality was the monstrously popular *Chappelle's Show*, which was created and co-written by two friends, one Black, Dave Chappelle, and one white, Neal Brennan, each of whom had tremendous respect for, interest in, and knowledge of, the other race's culture. Neal Brennan, speaking about himself and Chappelle, told me, "We were both pretty racially ambidexterous.

Just from pure exposure and interest. I'm as inspired by Spike Lee as Dave is by Kurt Cobain." In the 1980s, we watched a recalibration of what it means to be Black in the collective American mind.

In 1989, author Trey Ellis published a now legendary essay called "The New Black Aesthetic," which talked about Blacks who had a multicultural fluency powering their work. "A cultural mulatto," Ellis wrote, "educated by a multi-racial mix of cultures, can also navigate easily in the white world. And it is by and large this rapidly growing group of cultural mulattoes that fuels the New Black Aesthetic. We no longer need to deny or suppress any part of our complicated and sometimes contradictory cultural baggage to please whites or Blacks. The culturally mulatto Cosby girls are equally as legitimately Black as a Black teenage welfare mother." Within this movement Ellis identifies "the initial shock troops," that is, the culture creators who are leading this charge. He names Eddie Murphy, Wynton and Branford Marsalis, and, of course, Prince. In a recent interview Ellis said, "Before, there would be a stigma for Black artists taking from white culture because we have such a sense of cultural supremacy to us so we'd think why are we gonna borrow from some inferior culture? But Prince says I'm gonna take from everybody and he was kind of, like, talking white through his guitar."

In this crossover-friendly era, when lots of Black artists were making work meant for the mainstream without risking their cred, Prince was pushing that envelope by emerging from the funk and soul of *Controversy* and *1999* into the sound of *Purple Rain*, which was rock, pop, funk, and soul all wrapped up in a much more mainstream-accessible sound than he'd ever made. Dickerson says he helped influence Prince to follow his muse into a sound that was more racially-mixed, a journey that he thinks really began with *Dirty Mind*.

Dickerson explained, "*Dirty Mind* was the creative collision of where he had come from and this emerging influence of new wave and punk and things he was being exposed—that I was actively exposing him to because that's what I was into. That was the energy I wanted to bring to the band. So, in *Dirty Mind* you start to see, sonically, there's a mélange of Black sounds and sounds that have traditionally been made by white musicians. Prince was generally a fan of a proud palette of music. He was a fan of Sly but also a fan of Graham Central Station and Santana and the Bar-Kays. So all of that music showed up in the stew. But none of it was an overt homage. It was meant to be a new flavor."

Alan Leeds told me some people's response to Prince's sound was confusion. "My generation [the boomers] said, who does he think he is? Tryin' to be white? But the younger age group, the Questloves and D'Angelos who were coming up, they didn't see it that way at all. They grew up looking at the music differently than previous generations because the walls were down and they embraced the music purely on quality as opposed to any kind of categorization. So, it was an evolutionary time and not just in the music—the music was reflecting the evolution of the culture at large." The rise of cultural crossover is synecdochic for the embrace of multiculturalism happening in society.

Few songs express the idea that Prince's identity is multifaceted, that he consists of multiple selves at once, as "Controversy." In many ways, it's about myth building. Prince is saying the world is asking about me, and he's feigning a lack of understanding as to why people are so interested in the nooks and crannies of his life. But "Controversy" was written before Prince was a superstar, so he's not truly responding to the question of "Who are you?" as much as activating a sense of mystery and intrigue about him. It's a classic marketing technique: He's making you wonder about him by telling you many others are wondering about him. Is he Black or white? Is he straight or gay? Does he believe in God or does he believe in himself? These are the key schisms of his art if not of his life—his race, his sexuality, and his egotism versus his humbling relationship to a higher power. These are issues he'll hash out in his music throughout his career.

This is an important song in the strategic effort to build Prince as a person who audiences should be thinking about as more than just a music maker, but as a personal liberator. Someone who rejects labels, thus giving you the freedom to live beyond them, too. He says, "I wish there were no Black or white, I wish there were no rules." And "Life is just a game, we're all just the same." This is the ethos of multiculturalism and utopianism set to music. Prince sits at the edges of race, gender, and sexuality and rejects all borders, saying what does it matter what my demographics are? Who cares about my personal stats? Let's just have fun.

In this, Prince was just the most overt of 1980s pop stars who were breaking down identity barriers in race and gender while working in multiple idioms and blurring old school lines about audiences. There were others playing with those lines as well, including Madonna, Michael Jackson, Boy George, and others. Of course, the particular way Prince was transgressing identity boundaries and refusing to be labeled and challenging assumed notions of race and gender was more fascinating to watch and a much more complicated game. He seemed to be simultaneously questioning what it meant to be Black and to be a man—all this with an unusual poise. He was crossing over in all sorts of ways, but really he wanted to avoid categorization altogether and be a genre unto himself sonically and interpersonally.

Musicologist Griffin Woodworth wrote about this in a 2008 dissertation called "Just Another One of God's Gifts: Prince, African-American Masculinity, and the Sonic Legacy of the Eighties." Woodworth writes, "If, as Stuart Hall famously wrote, gender is the modality through which race is lived, then even as Prince was creating songs that invited the audience to imagine different ways of experiencing sexual pleasure, or what life would be like outside of the binary opposition between man and woman, he was simultaneously shadowboxing with the 'superspade' archetype that dragged down Hendrix and disarticulating the idioms of funk and soul music from the clichéd (or stereotyped) expectations of Black masculinity that had arisen in the 1970s. . . . Prince has mobilized all of the tools of African-American musical culture for the purpose of escaping the repressive modes of representation that have clung to African-American identity."[3]

So, just as he's demonstrated a rare fluidity to slide between rock, soul, pop, and funk, a sonic code switching that has helped him defy categorization and rise to the top of the segregated music industry, Prince has also used his fluency in a plethora of identity idioms to break free of the conventions and strictures of Black male identity. Prince becomes successful because his message is so attractive to so many: that identity is fluid, that gender and race are not defined boxes, but are malleable enough to let someone sit inside and outside them at the same time and be whatever they want to be. And he presents this message at the moment in history when many people most need to hear it. In *Prince: The Making of a Pop Music Phenomenon*, Stan Hawkins and Sarah Niblock write, "During the neo-conservative Reagan era, monogamy and gender fixity and adherence to religious doctrines and being defined by ethnicity were being promoted heavily and he said that all had to be broken for the sake of inner integrity. Prince was telling us that we are all the originators of our own destinies as long as we access our inner essence. In a society that was marked by high unemployment and the very real prospect of nuclear war, Prince was offering a safe space for his fans to explore the meanings of their own identities and their place within a confusing socio-cultural context."[4]

The song that most effectively communicates Prince's feelings about multiculturalism and diversity and seeing beyond demographics and labels is "Uptown" from *Dirty Mind*, another story song that's pornish but is also politically significant: Dickerson described it as Prince's manifesto of racial freedom. He's walking down the streets of a place he calls "your fine city," but Dickerson confirmed that it's meant to be Minneapolis, which many residents feel is something of a multiracial oasis that is extremely liberal and accepting of difference. Alan Leeds called it "the miscegenation capital of the world. I don't know the numbers but it sure feels like that."

In "Uptown," a woman beckons Prince and asks him if he's gay, thus defining her as a person who's trying to label people. Prince responds by asking her if she is, but this is just a way of exposing her question as ridiculous. He says to himself, "She's just a crazy, crazy, crazy little mixed-up dame. She's just a victim of society. And all its games." Again he's referring to demographics and isms as "games." In his mind, she's confused—she's someone who believes labels are relevant ways of distinguishing people. He knows better. He sings, "Now where I come from / We don't let society / Tell us how it's supposed to be." He's liberated from society's dogmatic reliance on labels. And he wants to take her to where he's from, a utopia that taught him to see people as people, to embrace diversity and reject essentialism—a place he calls "uptown." A place where "White, Black, Puerto Rican / Everybody just a-freakin'." Soon after they make love—of course—signifying how Prince has won her over and turned her on to his way of thinking and away from labelism. Then he says, "Now, where I come from / We don't give a damn / We do whatever we please / It ain't about no downtown / nowhere bound / narrow-minded drag / It's all about bein' free."

Prince embodies gen X multiculturalism, not only by sonically trafficking in funk and soul as well as rock and pop but also by making his bands Black and white, male and female. This is important and distinct and a conscious choice that says much about Prince. The Revolution (like the Family Stone and the E Street Band) were demographically mixed, but most bands come from one demographic quadrant: They're all white men or all Black men or all white women or all Black women. Sure, there are a few bands that have one Black or Asian or Latino member—Guns N' Roses, The Jimi Hendrix Experience, Smashing Pumpkins, or Sade (which is the name of the band). Some bands are mixed gender—Sade, Fleetwood Mac, the Pretenders, the Fugees, Arcade Fire, Superchunk, Cults, the Kills, Sleigh Bells, the White Stripes, Beach House, Belle & Sebastian, Of Montreal, Dead Weather, and others. As you can see from that list, many indie rock bands have both genders. However, most bands are composed of one race and one gender: U2, REM, De La Soul, TLC, Run-DMC, NWA, Coldplay, Radiohead, Destiny's Child, the Rolling Stones, the Beatles, 4 Non-Blondes, the Red Hot Chili Peppers, Led Zeppelin, Sleater-Kinney, Living Colour, The National, The Wu-Tang Clan, The Police, the Smiths, the Strokes, Sonic Youth, Public Enemy, Talking Heads, A Tribe Called Quest, Vampire Weekend, and many others; I could go on forever. All this may have something to do with how bands tend to start.

"Most bands," Questlove said, "come from high school or neighborhood experiences." At that age, for many people, most of your friends look like you. But there may be more to it. The tribal nature of being in a band was addressed in the U2 documentary, *From the Sky Down*. At the beginning of the film, a voice says: "What people are doing when they're forming a band is forming what anthropologists would call forming a clan, a group of people who may not be genetically related but share interests of some kind and have pledged loyalty to each other."[5] So, they are a sort of tribe, or gang, who've come to give you cool and thrills and soul and sound in an attempt to conquer their poverty and/or celibacy and general mediocrity, boredom, and lameness.

There's a primal hunter-gatherer nature to the band experience: They must go out in public and figuratively slay audience after audience. These are situations in which the band may feel like it's kill or be killed, especially when the band's unsure that it's going to make it. A group of people banding together to interact with audiences that may or may not be hostile or indifferent would probably feel the need to surround themselves with people they're comfortable going into conflict with, like a band of brothers. Or sisters.

These groups are in many ways laying their lives on the line; at the early stages of their career they may sacrifice traditional career advancement, relationships, a trustworthy flow of money, and creature comforts like consistent beds, all for the pleasure of spending years traveling around in a van and staying in crappy hotels and making very little money in pursuit of a dream. They must make a commitment to being music makers before they know if it'll work out for them and it does not work out for the vast majority of them. Seventy-seven thousand albums were released in 2011. Only forty-eight sold more than five hundred thousand. Only thirteen sold more than 1 million. Very few musicians make real money from music. Carrie Brownstein of Sleater-Kinney once said being in a successful indie band might open you up to well-paying secondary opportunities, but being in a successful band is not in and of itself an endeavor that is well paying. (She's not even mentioning all the moderately successful, barely successful, and unsuccessful bands.)

So, when you're risking your life to achieve your dream, and risking your pride performing in front of people you don't know in cities you barely know, I can see where you would find it helpful to feel surrounded by like-minded soldiers and, in many cases, that means people from the same demographic. That said, it's telling that Prince attacked the problem of forming the band he needed to help him conquer the world in the inverse way. He insisted on having bands that are multicultural and bigendered. Why? Because he knew it would help propel his career.

The structure of Prince's bands reflects both 1980s multiculturalism and a 1960s utopianism—they purposely recall Sly and the Family Stone. "Cats had to fit with the look he wanted, not the sound," Questlove says. "He didn't pick the best players, he picked people who fit with his multicultural vision. The plan was always to have two white male members, two females, and two Black members, and he would've been one of those Black people. He wanted an updated Sly and the Family Stone thing."

Dickerson, who was in those early bands, confirmed that Prince was overtly thinking about the diversity of the band when casting it. "Absolutely, it was a conscious thing," he said. "In fact, there were some folks that we auditioned that didn't get the nod because they didn't fit the branding template that he had in mind: multiracial, male and female." Eric Leeds said, "There were women in the band who were lesbians. There were whites and Blacks in the band and several of us who were Jewish in the band. There was this image he was trying to present to the world that it's not about the differences in us so let's celebrate the diversity." What was that about? Partly, it was about the musical heritage of Minneapolis. "The Twin Cities had always been a place where you had multiracial bands that did a wide variety of music. That had always been a part of the fabric of the town musically." However, perhaps the real reason that Prince insisted on a multiracial band is he knew that being onstage with a diverse group of people was good branding and it would help protect him from music business segregation.

Marylou Badeaux, a Warner Bros. executive, told a Prince biographer that Prince made it clear to them he did not want to be ghettoized. "Prince was very concerned about being labeled a Black artist or being segmented into the Black department. He said to us, 'I'm not an R&B artist. I'm not a rock 'n' roller. I'm an artist and I do a wide range of music. If I deliver you rock 'n' roll, don't come back to me and say I can't do it because I'm Black." [6] According to Howard Bloom, one of Prince's early managers, it was a fight for Prince to get out of the racial box. "From the start, the record industry had conceived of Prince as a young Stevie Wonder or Smokey Robinson, not a rare, Hendrixlike figure who could traverse boundaries. Prince was a Black artist [and] would encounter significant resistance from Warner Bros. when he tried to change this perception." [7]

His desire to be marketed and promoted by the pop-music staff challenged the music business status quo in which most major labels had Black music departments built to help market and promote to Black media and consumers. Those Black music departments were usually less well funded and had smaller staffs than the pop-music department, leaving them in a world of separate and unequal. Prince understood the business and wanted to access the pop music staff and their larger marketing and promotion budget rather than the smaller resources allocated for marketing and promoting Black music for pragmatic reasons.

"He understood the segregation of the industry," Alan Leeds told me. "He said, I have to position myself so they can't treat me that way, they can't categorize the music that way. I have to have white people in the band and girls in the band. Sly had the right idea. I'm gonna do what Sly did and they're gonna cross me over, otherwise I'll forever be the Black artist. He said, whatever you do, don't allow yourself to be typecast in the R&B ghetto because then you'll forever be just that." He wanted to reach for the large mainstream audience and not the smaller audience that came along with being identified as being a Black star.

"You have to make [your band] look like America to make it in America," a wise old musician told Questlove when he was a child. "When you form that band make sure you put a white boy in the group. And a woman. And then you won't have to do this Chitlin' Circuit bullshit. Maybe you'll get farther than we did." Questlove said Prince knew that his band would have a brighter future if it looked as diverse as America and that was crucial to him because people who know about Prince's early years say he was obsessed with not having to go through the traditional Black music road. "Part of Prince's resistance to doing his first national tour with Rick James was, I don't want to have to ride this Chitlin' Circuit wave just to make a way in the world. He also made a conscious decision to reject going on *Soul Train* because that's seen as the Chitlin' Circuit route." He didn't want to be a Black star but a star who happened to be Black.

One of Prince's early managers aimed to solve that challenge by having Prince's first tour consist of doing two shows in each city, first opening for a funk group, then performing in a new wave club. But Prince had more tricks up his sleeve than an integrated band and a mixed touring schedule: Prince lied to early interviewers about being biracial: In 1981, he told Nelson George, then a reporter for *Record World*, that his mother was white, and told Bill Adler, who was writing about him for *Rolling Stone*, that he was the "son of a half-black father and an Italian mother." [8] Prince pushed this further along by casting a white woman to play his mother in *Purple Rain*. (Despite lingering rumors, Prince is not mixed: Both of his parents were Black.) He said he was biracial because he knew that being perceived as mixed would open his possibilities and keep him from being forced into the Black music box. This can be seen as a sort of passing, albeit passing for mixed. Prince was attempting to break out of the box into which American society would have placed his Black body in order to liberate himself. Alan Leeds said Prince consciously rebelled against being typecast or limited and this was one of the ways to do it. Prince was passing as biracial for the same reason some Blacks have, throughout history, passed for white: to attempt to sidestep racism and access the benefits of white-skin privilege or at least to acquire the freedom and power over his destiny that often springs from white-skin privilege. He realized that being seen as Black could be confining for him: He would be subject to smaller record company budgets and smaller audiences while playing within the institutions of Black culture while being seen as mixed would liberate him from "the Chitlin' Circuit route," and could turn him from a Black artist into an artist, helping him access the largest possible budgets, audiences, and stages. It was about Prince insisting on having access to the full breadth of human possibility.

Passing, historically, is about effectively becoming white. Some people took advantage of their whitelike appearance and escaped to an area where no one knew their family and their past so they could be perceived as white and live as if they were white. Passing is not about hating Blackness but about giving yourself the best possible chance in life. It's about refusing to allow white supremacy's harsh judgment of Black potential to constrain your life's journey. It's about fooling the society that would punish Blackness and exploiting a loophole in the system. But we know that Prince certainly didn't want to squander the Blackest impulses inside him; they were in his music and in his side projects. Questlove said, "He created [the band] the Time to satisfy that part of himself. In the Time he saw himself as a pimp. And a nigga." Eric Leeds told the *Minneapolis Star Tribune*, "The Time was basically his way of making R&B music without being pigeonholed as an R&B artist."[9] In *Possessed*, Alex Hahn wrote of even deeper psychic itches that The Time helped Prince scratch, saying elements of Morris Day's character were borrowed from Prince's father. "When Prince began to record music for the project," Hahn wrote, "he sang the guide vocals (which would later be imitated by Day note-for-note) in a raspy voice that sounded like an old man. 'That was him imitating his dad and men of his father's generation—barber shop guys,' noted Susan Rogers."[10]

In terms of gender hiring Prince was progressive, living out multiculturalism by consistently placing women in his band and putting them outside the traditional tokenist roles that women in bands so often get, like bass guitar. After his first album, he formed a band that had Gayle Chapman on keyboards. A few years later, he formed the Revolution, which would have Lisa Coleman on keys and piano and Wendy Melvoin on guitar. Later he put Sheila E. on drums. Far from pure eye candy, they were significant contributors to the band. This list could also include Peggy McCreary and Susan Rogers who, though not players, were engineers, an important role in an area in which there are few women. Rogers was hired despite being young and having minimal professional experience and she lasted through Prince's most fertile period, from *Purple Rain* to *Sign "O" the Times*.

Interestingly, Prince allowed his struggle to take Wendy and Lisa seriously as musicians and writers to be an important subtext in *Purple Rain*, the movie. The guy who consistently had women contributing musically in his bands presented himself as a sexist bandleader for most of the movie until the end, when he accepts Wendy and Lisa's music. Eric Leeds said, "The plotline is he wouldn't allow Wendy and Lisa to contribute to the band and then after he goes through all the crisis with his family, he opens himself up to allow them to come into him with a song. You can look at 'Purple Rain' as redemption. He got his redemption in the end by being able to open himself up. Because the whole thing is here's this really self-absorbed, insular artist who isn't going to allow himself to open up to any influence whatsoever."

This subtext of Prince's primarily dismissive, but ultimately respectful, relationship with Wendy and Lisa also represents a struggle over whether or not these women will have artistic agency in rock, which is often a battle. Female musicians who have record deals and are in the studio working on their own albums have told me about sessions of theirs where the music they write is disrespected and dismissed by the men around them to such an extent that they find themselves in tears. Prince mimics, and activates, some of this sexism throughout the movie. For instance, Prince's father in the movie is physically abusive toward his mother and, eventually, Prince, in a fit of rage, strikes Apollonia, perpetuating the common cycle of kids who grow up seeing domestic violence eventually repeating it. But Prince worships women and does not want to become his father, so he repents. Part of his redemption, it seems, is to go into his true family, his band, and give respect to Wendy and Lisa. He embraces their music, reworks their song, and in the climactic performance, the Revolution finally performs a Wendy and Lisa song onstage. It's "Purple Rain," and it kills. It's his aesthetic zenith in the film, the moment where he most deeply connects with the audience and wins the ongoing battle of the bands.

Of course the movie's portrayal of the genesis of "Purple Rain" is a Hollywoodization. Prince wrote the song without significant help. Matt Fink confirmed that Wendy and Lisa didn't write the skeleton of the song we see in *Purple Rain*. "Prince wrote the lyric and melody to that chord progression," he said. "He presented that to us in rehearsal. From a lyric and melody standpoint that's all Prince." Fink, who played on "Purple Rain," said in the context of the movie the song was like an "apology to Wendy and Lisa. Look, here it is, I wrote the song around the music you presented, which is now 'Purple Rain.'" Was it realistic that Prince wasn't listening to anyone in the band but came around to hearing Wendy and Lisa? Fink says yes. "Probably in a lot of ways he was aware of that reality," Fink told me. "He had his vision. He had to write his stuff and do what he wanted and then he was still ambivalent about including the band into his vision as writers, but later he had a much more fruitful relationship with Wendy and Lisa as far as cowriting compared to anyone else in the group." I'm told that there are recordings of him doing Wendy and Lisa songs that remain in the vaults.

The inspiration for the song "Purple Rain" came from a place no one would have guessed. Prince's 1999 Tour followed Bob Seger's tour through America. (The Silver Bullet Band is another mixed gender group.) Seger and Prince played many of the same cities within a few nights of each other and Prince didn't understand the success of the rock star who was then much bigger than he. He wondered, *What does he have that I don't?* He ended up talking to Matt Fink about it. "I was with Prince after a show," Fink said, "and we were hanging out at the arena where Seger was performing and Prince asked me what made Seger so successful and I said well he plays really straight ahead mainstream white rock and roll. If you created a song like that you'd get even bigger. That was my advice to him and I think it influenced him to write a song like 'Purple Rain' which is very mainstream-y, not funky, it's a ballad, it sounds like it could be a country song almost. So, I really think that statement I gave him definitely could have influenced him. I don't know for sure but I think he took it to heart." I'm told by several people that Prince spent some time obsessing over Seger's stadium songs, those big-sounding, easy-to-sing-along-with anthems that speak to deep, basic emotions that unite people. Songs like "Roll Me Away," "We've Got Tonight," and "Against the Wind."

Listening to Seger, Prince figured out how to write his own power ballad and came up with "Purple Rain." "It's telling," Questlove said, "that Prince purposely toned down the record as he worked on it, taking 90 percent of the sexuality out of it, knowing that would ruin his moment." But what is "Purple Rain" about? It's about salvation. Redemption. Deliverance. Classic Christian themes. This, even though it's an oblique song that's short on lyrics. It begins: "I never meant to cause you any sorrow." The speaker's at that painful moment that we've all known: The relationship is ending and the melancholy vibe of the power ballad signals something painfully bittersweet. But it's not over because the narrator is a bad person: He may have caused her pain but he never meant to and still doesn't. His heart was always in the right place. This is Prince, as the auteur, absolving the speaker. Questlove explains, "This is a narrative about forgiveness so bathing in the 'Purple Rain' could be a spiritual baptism of sorts. Not that he's speaking in regret prose but the lyrics speak to, 'I wanna put whatever differences we have behind us and I just want what's best for you. I only wanna see you bathing in the Purple Rain.'" Wendy Melvoin, a guitarist in the Revolution, once told a reporter, "I think the song represents a change in someone's life, a good change. It means freedom to me. The whole idea of 'Purple Rain' is that it's mystical." [11]

What sort of relationship was it? The second verse seems to suggest it was perhaps a friendship that blossomed into an affair or was on the lip of becoming a full-blown affair. Prince says, "I never wanted to be your weekend lover," and "I could never steal you from another." But the lines following those two are about friendship which speaks to the intimacy the speaker truly wanted out of the relationship, that same sort of urge for closeness rather than sex that characterizes "If I Was Your Girlfriend." That speaks to the purity of the speaker's desire. He only wanted to be some kind of friend. His desire is virtuous. And that makes the song cleansing, something baptismal. We all would love to have such grace and forgiveness in the difficult final moments of a relationship and, here, Prince allows us to feel it. Of course, the song is also part of the effort to position Prince as a Jesus figure. More than just loving God and making Him a central part of his music, Prince occasionally slips into wanting you to think of him as Jesuslike. Actually, it's more than occasionally. Fans who paid close attention could feel Prince's winking acknowledgment that he was their savior and that he may have thought of himself as a Messiah.

3

I'm Your Messiah

GENERATION X'S SKEPTICISM and cynicism extended to all institutions, including religion. Ours was a secular generation that had less religious engagement than any before it. A 2010 PEW Forum poll found only a fifth of gen Xers attended a religious service each week, down from a quarter of boomers, and that 21 percent of gen Xers were "religiously unaffiliated," far more than boomers (13 percent) and members of the silent generation (6 percent). In the introduction to Tom Beaudoin's *Virtual Faith,* Harvey Cox, Jr., from the Harvard Divinity School wrote, "Their religious proclivities have remained a mystery almost as inscrutable as that of the Holy Trinity. Here is a generation that stays away from most churches in droves but loves songs about God and Jesus, a generation that would score very low on any standard piety scale but at times seems almost obsessed with saints, visions, and icons in all shapes and sizes." That makes sense to me. Several religious scholars agreed that the impulse to worship is baked deep into the human soul, and that the spiritual imperative is a natural urge. All of us have a need to believe in something, which is why religion has flourished on every continent for many centuries. In a time of waning religious engagement, gen Xers still had to fulfill their worship needs somewhere. The answer for many was to become worshipful of celebrities.

In *Virtual Faith*, Beaudoin writes that gen X was religious but in an unconventional way. "[My] fundamental claim [is] generation X is—despite and even because of appearances—strikingly religious. We express our religious interests, dreams, fears, hopes, and desires through popular culture." For many, their religious impulse was fulfilled by worshipping a musician. Music writer Rob Sheffield once said, "Being a pop fan is a lot like Catholic devotion . . . lots of ritual, lots of ceremony . . . we touch the icon to enter the sacred space, genuflecting to reliquaries and ostentatoria that make something splendid of our most secret desires and agonies." Musicians sometimes capitalize on the fans' desire to worship by creating concerts that resemble a revival tent, with a focus on a shamanistic leader who invokes mass ecstasy and stars who present themselves as updated religious icons. Think of Elvis, James Brown, George Clinton, Jim Morrison, Robert Plant, David Bowie, Madonna, and, of course, Prince. He packed his music with religious messages and gospel tropes but, more than that, was the best in history at articulating himself as a pop star who is a Jesus figure. So much so that some, including those close to him, wondered if he thought he was some sort of Messiah.

"There was a running subtext when I was in the band," Dez Dickerson told me, "a theme of 'We were sent to help people see.' That was a recurring theme. Not in the music but in the inner conversation of the band that he initiated. He didn't have this overt, I'm Jesus, thing. It was this sense that there was a certain enlightenment that he, and we, by default, were messengers of and we were there to bring this enlightenment to people who needed it. That was part of the musical mission. So, why the Lord's Prayer in the middle of 'Controversy'? There's some redemptive purpose in exposing people to the Lord's Prayer in the middle of this other jam. Because we are the messengers of some higher level of understanding in the guise of punk-funk or whatever the hell we were doing. He had a sense of being called, if you will. Of being a special messenger of some sort. And, frankly, he had people at different intervals who told him that."

Dickerson revealed to Dave Hill, author of *Pop Life*, that one of those people telling Prince that he was special was Gayle Chapman. "It didn't help that Gayle was telling him that he was blessed by God with some special dispensation. He sort of ate all this up."[1] I asked Chapman if she told Prince he was blessed by God. She said she did. But, she also said she told everyone that. "I might have told him he was blessed by God simply because he was," she said. "So was I. It wasn't because of anything special in particular. That's what God does, in my belief." Some think Prince may have taken her words about God blessing him to heart and embraced it so tightly that others may have believed it, too. Eric Leeds said, "There was always this feeling that in his own particular way he had the inside track. Once we were playing an outdoor concert in Japan and it was threatening to rain and we were all concerned about having to play a gig in the rain and one of the guys on the crew just laughed and said, 'Oh, no, it's not gonna rain. Prince will talk to his buddy upstairs and make sure it doesn't rain.' That night it drizzled. Not enough to disrupt anything."

Dickerson said Prince's relationship with God was real and serious, though it was also one of the many parts of him. "There's maybe three Prince personas," Dickerson said. "One of them is a very calculated marketing mind. That's where the 'embodying pure sex' thing comes from. Another of them is 'I'm gonna be the baddest musician there ever was.' And then there's the guy who really is thoughtful and introspective and holds religious considerations close to his heart and ponders those questions sincerely and genuinely and deeply. And those are the three guys who, over the years, have vied for the microphone."

Did Prince really think he was a sort of messiah? Well, in many places he asserts just that. "I Would Die 4 U" is a song that makes plain the crucial similarity between the speaker and Jesus: to die for someone means your devotion to them is equivalent to Jesus's devotion to us. More, the song is filled with allusions to Jesusness. In the first verse he says, "If you're evil I'll forgive you by and by." Jesus is forgiving of evil. In the third verse Prince sings, "I'm not a human. I'm a dove. I'm your conscious. I am love." The dove is often used as a symbol of the Holy Spirit. Christians also refer to their consciousness as the voice of the Holy Spirit. And Jesus, we are often told by Christianity, is love. So, three times in a short burst Prince is aligning himself with a member of the Holy Trinity. In the second verse Prince comes right out with it and says, "I'm your messiah." Is Prince singing in the voice of Jesus or does he want us to think he is the second coming?

Questlove, who has studied both Prince's music and Christian music, explains, "I think in his mind he was lending voice to what he perceived as being the gospel message. I don't think he's literally saying he's the messiah but in his own way he's speaking for the messiah. That's a lyrical device that, if you look at gospel music and contemporary Christian music, that's a common club in the bag. That's a consistent lyrical device. A lot of Christian songs have you singing in the voice of God and Prince takes advantage of that."

Dickerson told me, "We're all capable of what I call that Balaam and the talking donkey moment. That's that Old Testament passage where God speaks through a donkey. In that moment, there's the instrumentality of Him interrupting some guy's choices and saying, well, I'm just gonna speak through this donkey. And, I think, every once in a while, we have a moment of brilliance where we create something profound. I think Prince had experienced something. I think he had a moving experience with respect to the idea of who Jesus is or was and he wanted to express it in a song. It's not a very cloaked lyric. It says what it says. He's saying he is Jesus."

Another song in which Prince is saying he's holy is "1999," his song about the apocalypse. In the song's first moments he distorts his vocal to speak in the voice of God: "Don't worry. I won't hurt you. I only want you to have some fun." It's fitting that God is present in the song because it's a vision of Judgment Day. The song begins, "I was dreamin' when I wrote this . . ." Dreams can also be the source of visions, which are often had by people who are celestially special. For Prince to speak of having a vision of Judgment Day is perhaps to place himself with the prophets of legend. But, what exactly is meant by what Prince as God says, "Don't worry, I won't hurt you. I only want you to have some fun"? In a song about the apocalypse, this seems a rather callous introductory statement: "Don't worry? I won't hurt you?" What are you talking about?! You're about to wipe the Earth clean! I'm very, very worried! But if you look at God on Judgment Day as Prince may have, based on his childhood religious education as a Seventh-Day Adventist, then the Earth is filled with sin and wickedness and, on the final day, God would be moving to cleanse and restore Earth to its original sinless state, which will make it possible for humanity to fulfill its spiritual potential and reach maximum enjoyment. Knowing that, you understand there's benevolence behind God saying, "I won't hurt you. I only want you to have some fun." He's saying, "You can trust me, this will help you. I want you to enjoy the Kingdom of Heaven. It's not the end of the world. It's the beginning of your real life." And what about "Don't worry?" A religious scholar pointed out to me that in the Bible, when God or an angel appears to someone the first thing said is usually something along the lines of, "Do not be afraid." *Don't worry* would fulfill that and also show Prince fashioning his message from God in the same form as the messages in the Bible, especially Revelations.

Even if you don't know or notice all the Biblical allusions, when Prince gives us his voice as the voice of God (which he also does in "Temptation" from *Around the World in a Day*), it subtly acculturates us into thinking of Prince as akin to God. He attempted this leger-demain before *Purple Rain*: the first film he tried to make was called *The Second Coming*. It fell apart before it could be finished, but we can still see his intention in the title. Naming a film about himself *The Second Coming* is a cheeky gesture, especially given that the movie did not attempt to present Prince as Jesuslike. Questlove says it was a concert film with a narrative about playing a homecoming show in Minnesota's largest venue. But Prince surely knew that title would be a lightning rod and would not-so-subtly activate the perception that he is like Jesus.

Prince does this sort of activating and alluding more aggressively in the last verse of "Purple Rain," his magnum opus, when he says, "You say you want a leader, but you can't seem to make up your mind. I think you better close it. And let me guide you. To the Purple Rain." What's he saying there? That's not him talking in the voice of God. He's talking about himself and telling us to accept him as our leader who we should allow to shepherd us into the rain. And what does the rain mean? Questlove tells me it's intended as a baptismal symbol. Water is often a symbol of baptism or rebirth.

For Prince to offer himself as a leader guiding us into the baptis-mal water in a song about redemption that absolves the narrator, is, I think, to once again posit himself as a Jesus figure. How many times can he say it and get away with the excuse of using the lyrical device of speaking in the voice of God and not actually speaking in his own voice? And what if he's draped his iconography in purple because it subtly links him to Christ? In the King James version of the Book of Mark, just before the crucifixion, it says, "And they clothed him with purple, and plaited a crown of thorns, and put it about his head, and began to salute him, Hail, King of the Jews! And they smote him on the head with a reed and did spit upon him and bowing their knees, worshipped him. And when they had mocked him, they took off the purple from him, and put his own clothes on him, and led him out to crucify him." So, wearing purple becomes yet another way of likening himself to Christ.

Being like Christ is about more than just being a spiritual leader. It's also about dealing with pain and betrayal: Jesus is a God who suffers and whose suffering is critical to his image and importance. He suffers because He is betrayed by people He trusts, including His Heavenly Father to whom he says, "My God, why have You forsaken me?" This sentiment shows up in "When Doves Cry": Prince speaks to his mother, asking why she has forsaken him when he says "How could you just leave me standing alone in a world that's so cold."

Maybe all this is simply the work of an ecstatic true believer spilling from the voice of a preacher into the voice of God. When the preacher is caught up in the spirit he's liable to say anything but we know he knows he's merely the conduit, and not God Himself, so we trust him wherever he goes. And Prince spends much time presenting himself as the greatest and most badass preacher that pop music has ever seen. "Let's Go Crazy" gives us Prince pretending to be in the pulpit while laying out his theology in the form of the coolest sermon ever heard on top-forty radio. A Baptist churchy organ riffs in the background as Prince preaches, "Dearly beloved, we are gathered here today to get through this thing called life." The sound of it all makes me feel like I'm in a little wooden church where Prince is in the pulpit, resplendent in a beautiful white suit filled with buttons. "Electric word life. It means forever and that's a mighty long time! But I'm here to tell you! There's something else . . . ! The afterworld!"

That sermon would fit in so many churches on so many Sunday mornings. It's Prince laying out his religious philosophy about the afterlife being a better world where you're not alone and where you're truly happy, as opposed to this world where people rely on expensive psychiatrists and medications to get themselves through. Prince told Chris Rock in their 1998 VH1 interview, " 'Let's Go Crazy' was about God and Satan. I had to change those words up but 'de-elevator' was Satan. I had to change those words up cuz you couldn't say God on the radio. Let's go crazy was God to me. Stay happy, stay focused, and you can beat the de-elevator." [2]

It's crucial that "Let's Go Crazy," which lays out Prince's theology, is *Purple Rain*'s first song; we begin with Prince literally in the pulpit. The album's last song is the title song, which is about redemption through baptism. In this way, the album sort of takes us through the structure of a religious event by opening with the preaching of the word and ending with the audience being forgiven and baptized.

"Let's Go Crazy," which is done in a tempo way faster than a normal R&B song—it more closely resembles an uptempo gospel song—is a joyful tune that sees Prince's spirit triumphant over the everyday pains of life. His religion has got him so indomitably happy that he refuses to be brought down when he calls his woman to say hello and discovers she's in the midst of cheating: "She picked up the phone, dropped it on the floor, ah, ah, is all I heard." He's filled with that irrepressible joy even in the face of pain that you see in highly religious folk. Prince knows you're relying on Dr. Everythingwillbealright and he knows that that quack can't really help you. He sings instead of asking him how much time is left in your session, why not get real and ask him how much of your mind is left? His meds can't save you.

Only God can. The tragicomic character Dr. Everythingwillbealright of Beverly Hills is the symbol for all the wrong things people rely on to get them through. What's Prince's answer? "Hang tough, children." Why? "He's comin'!" Prince chants. "He's comin'!" It turns into a rock 'n' roll sermon. Now, I see Prince onstage at some purple-drenched megachurch in Minneapolis, preaching with his guitar strapped on, ecstatically yelling above his cheering, standing congregation: "He's comin!!! He's COMIN!!!" Then he busts out an incendiary guitar solo and looks to the sky and addresses Him directly with the song's last line: "Take me away!" He wants to go to this great Heaven right now. We kinda want to go with him.

Musicologist Griffin Woodworth's 2008 UCLA dissertation says "Let's Go Crazy" and its final guitar solo is dripping with gospel tropes. Woodworth calls the song's refrain, "Let's go crazy," a reference to ecstatic Pentecostalism and says Prince "celebrates gospel's influence in melody and structure. He mixed gospel and straight-up funk with the timbre, technology and iconography of rock guitar heroism."[3] For Woodworth, and for me, the entire song recalls high-energy gospel, but the extraordinary final guitar solo—where Prince reminds us he is a guitar god—takes us into the feeling of the Black church experience.

In a conversation we had, Woodworth told me, "Often you'll have a repetitive vamp in a fast gospel number where the choir is repeating a fragment of the chorus while the soloist interjects increasingly virtuosic vocal riffs. This kind of back-and-forth between soloist and choir is what heats up the congregation and helps draw the spirit down into the room and that moment of getting the spirit can be signaled in the music by one of those loud, high sustained wailing notes from the soloist. In the section leading up to the final guitar solo in 'Let's Go Crazy' Prince abandons the verse/chorus structure and has the band vamp on a short excerpt of the song's chord progression for nearly a minute during which his guitar plays an increasingly dynamic game of call-and-response with the background vocalists. This builds up the intensity until finally the rest of the band stops and Prince's guitar soars up to a long, high climactic pitch. Prince's virtuosic guitar solo at the end sounds like the moment of transcendence in a gospel song when the spirit moves within the congregation." He says the song has a structure typical of a gospel song, especially the ". . . climax in which the soloist has a transcendent moment and soars up to a long, sustained high note. This 'release' enacts the collapse of personal boundaries upon the joyful descent of the holy spirit, a moment enacted in Prince's performance by guitar glossolalia, a screaming microtonal pitch bend." He's saying the way Prince plays that solo recalls someone being overcome by the spirit and speaking in tongues.

Prince breathes several gospel tropes into "1999," the first time in his music that he really takes us to church, giving us both his end-time philosophy and the structures of Pentecostalist or Holiness worship. After the last verse, the song flows into a slew of voices that sound a bit like a messy chorus. An ecstatic call and response breaks out that almost recalls the zenith of a Pentecostalist service. The deep God voice we hear at the beginning returns here, rhythmically intoning "1999," almost as if He's kind of dancing with the people. Prince sings, "Don't you wanna go?" as if saying to us, "Don't y'all wanna go to the end of days!?" He's looking forward to Heaven and beckoning others to come with him. Then Prince changes his vocal a bit and adds a note of anxiety and fear into another voice that responds, "I don't wanna die! I'd rather dance my life away!" This is another person, perhaps representing a diversity of opinions in the congregation or the world or maybe even the duality within Prince. The first Prince voice responds, "Listen to what I'm tryin' to say!" as if urging the nonbelievers to take his message seriously. This happens as the chorus swells and amid the call and response the voices grow harder to sort out. The repeated refrain changes from "1999" to "party!" and it's a party all right—they're celebrating the end of days because it's time to go to Heaven. Prince, in the first voice, the one beckoning them to go, says, "Can't run from Revelation, no!" thus finishing the conversation with the anxious one by reminding us that the end of days is inevitable and referencing the book of Revelation which is so important to Adventism. The call and response then builds in energy until it's capped by Prince's long transcendent scream growing up then bursting above all other sounds like someone overcome by the spirit as in the climax of a gospel song or a Black church service. Questlove says, "The fire and brimstone ad libbing here is so gospel it's not funny."

Woodworth notes gospel tropes dancing throughout Prince's toolbox, but especially his trademark ecstatic falsetto scream. "These vocal pyrotechnics are a gospel music idiom that enacts the experience of divine ecstasy," he told me. "Prince's music is indebted to the model of sacred sexuality that, filtered through previous generations of R&B and soul singers, is the legacy of the worship practices of the Black Pentecostal and Holiness churches." Prince grew up in the first generation to have gospel tropes be widely dispersed into popular music. The ecstatic scream of transcendence and the male falsetto and the use of gospel structures in worldly music characterized much of the sounds Prince grew up listening to, like James Brown, Aretha Franklin, Stevie Wonder, Marvin Gaye, Al Green, and Curtis Mayfield. No longer did you need to go to church to hear gospel tropes, now they were inescapable in pop music and you would encounter them whether or not you went to church.

Prince's scream at the end of "1999" recalls screams heard in the Black church and screams and yells heard in the music of James Brown and Little Richard, both of whom were, of course, borrowing from the Black church. This is part of Malcolm Gladwell's point in *Outliers* about historical timing and how the moment in which we grow up shapes us: Prince's use of gospel and Black church tropes in his music is a product of their explosion in popular music in his youth and in this way, we can see the historical moment of his youth imprinting on him.

One of the central features of gospel is that ecstatic climactic scream that recalls both religious transcendence and sexual orgasm. It usually comes after the singer has left the structure of the music and even seems to have left behind the boundaries of language: At that point, they leap over the highest pitch that we've heard in the music to give us a high, long-sustained note that represents the spirit entering the body and lifting it up to a place of transcendence and superhuman ecstasy. If it's done authentically, it seems as if the singer could not have reached that height, that superhuman place, without being here and now in this church and with the choir pushing him and the spirit in his body lifting him. That's what so thrilling and affirming to the congregation—that they can see the spirit entering someone and working on them and pushing them up to a place of superhuman strength that they could not have reached without the aid of the spirit. It tells the congregation that through faith and the spirit we all can find the superhuman strength needed to get through the tribulations of life, especially Black life in America. Some scholars call this the "gettin' over" moment, I prefer to call it the "gettin' the spirit" moment, and it's as much a major part of Black American music experience as it is a part of the Black church musical experience.

The first time we ever heard the "gettin' the spirit" moment in Prince's music was in "Do Me, Baby" from *Controversy*. One might think finding gospel tropes in an overtly sexual song called "Do Me, Baby" to be sacrilegious, but that collision is a common feature of Black music. The singing in "Do Me, Baby" mimics gospel structure most distinctly in the third and fourth minutes of the song where you hear just the soloist, Prince, and the backup singers. First, Prince stays in the pocket and repeats fragments that the soloist can play off. As they do, the lead male falsetto leaves the structure of the music and soars farther and farther over the highest point previously reached in the song, giving us a succession of superhuman wailing screams in an ecstasy that resembles both sexual climax and religious transcendence. He's outside the structure of the song, and also outside the ability to speak English because he's so overcome with the spirit. His long moment of superhuman screams belongs equally in a bedroom or in front of a choir at the climactic moment of service. This is the getting the spirit moment par excellence.

We hear more of Prince giving us versions of this—Questlove calls it "fire-and-brimstone screams"—in various degrees toward the end of "1999," "When Doves Cry," "International Lover," "Computer Blue," "Darling Nikki," "The Beautiful Ones," "Kiss," "Little Red Corvette," "Adore," and, perhaps most ecstatically with his guitar, "Let's Go Crazy," where he seems to approximate speaking in tongues. Eric Leeds said, "When a song *really* meant something to him he would just inhabit it, much like a gospel singer would. Whether the source is spiritual or secular, when you feel it, you feel it."

So much of Prince's catalog is ready to be played in church on Sunday: his 1985 song "4 The Tears In Your Eyes" tells the story of Jesus as reverently and beautifully as any pop song ever has: "Long ago, there was a man. Change stone to bread with the touch of his hand. Made the blind see and the dumb understand." (It never appeared on an album but was included on his collection *The Hits/The B-Sides*.) "The Cross" from 1987's *Sign "O" the Times* is a hymn: "Don't cry, He is coming. Don't die without knowing the cross." The 1984 song "God" pulls from the story of creation. (It was the B-side to the single, "Purple

Rain," and did not appear on any album but the collection.) "And God Created Woman," from the *Symbol* album, also retells the story of Adam and Eve. "I Wish You Heaven," from 1988's *LoveSexy*, does little more than sweetly repeat that Christian pleasantry. 1996's *Emancipation* gives us "The Holy River," and this bit of preaching: "And then it hit 'cha like a fist on a wall. Who gave U life when there was none at all? Who gave the sun permission 2 rise up every day? Let me tell it. If U ask God 2 love U longer, every breath U take will make U stronger. Keepin U happy and proud 2 call His name. Jesus!" There's unreleased songs like "Evolsidog" (God is love backwards), and "God Is Alive." Also, "A Place In Heaven" from the *Black Album*, which speaks more deeply of Heaven and how difficult it is to get there: "She wants a place in Heaven, but she cannot face the truth. . . . We all want a place in Heaven. Suites of that level are few. Let's not be lazy, there's no room service, it's all up 2 me and U."

"Parade" is bookended by the discussion of Christopher Tracy, which is a barely coded name for Christ. The album concludes with the ballad "Sometimes It Snows In April," referencing the month that Christ was crucified, which is significant, because in the song we learn the man Prince calls Tracy has died and gone to Heaven. Prince sings, "He's better off than He was before. A whole lot better off than the fools He left here. . . . Maybe one day I'll see my Tracy again."

Prince's focus on religion is so tenacious that he allows religious messages to intrude in some of his most sexual songs, which suggests that even when he's thinking about sex he's unable to stop thinking about religion. Or that, after he's captured your attention via sex, he'll use the moment to slide in a note about God. But the combination of sex and spirituality within one song also, perhaps, suggests free associative thinking, letting the creative mind drift away from lust to land on whatever it may and, of course, that's God, because deep down that's what Prince's mind is truly focused on. Near the conclusion of "Dar-

ling Nikki," that pornish lust-filled tale, perhaps Prince's most lascivious song, the music segues into the sound of rain and wind and the
singing is played in reverse and he sings: "Hello, how are you? I'm fine
cause I know that the Lord is coming soon." In "Let's Pretend We're
Married," from *1999*, Prince gives us a sexual romp. It begins "Excuse
me but I need a mouth like yours, to help me forget the girl that just
walked out my door." But it concludes: "I'm in love with God, He's
the only way, cuz you and I know we gotta die some day . . . I'm goin
to another life. How about you?" There's also "Controversy," which
pauses in the middle of Prince talking about himself, and building
or speaking to myths about himself, to give us the Lord's Prayer done
without irony. He had been asking, in the song, "Do I believe in God?
Do I believe in me?" Segueing into the Lord's Prayer would answer
the question, saying we're all God's children and in God's eyes we're
all equal. It doesn't matter what your eyes tell you about me, we all
belong to God.

"Adore" also gives us this collision of the spiritual and the profane,
and does so in a more direct and visual way. In the second verse of the
epic love slash lust song, which is a seminal part of his oeuvre, Prince
says, "When we be makin 'love, I only hear the sounds, Heavenly
angels cryin up above. Tears of joy pourin' down on us. They know
we need each other." So, he's having passionate sex with her beneath
an audience of angels who look down approvingly, more than approv-
ing; they're welled up with emotion at how beautiful this moment
is. They're not peeping toms, they're saying it's celestially, spiritually,
and morally okay to be having steamy, intense, lustful lovemaking
because it's serious: He's having this incredible sex with her as a way
of showing his love. The song comes down to the idea with which it
started: "I'll be there for U until the end of time." This, for Prince, is
no idle statement: The end of time is a very real idea for him. Judgment day is something he's preparing for and more than that, death

is just a portal into another life, so the end of time stretches on into Heaven and into eternity meaning this is sex consecrating a love that will last forever.

This comingling of the profane and the spiritual is an age-old Black music trope. Quite often in Black music history the erotic and the divine, or the concerns of Saturday night and Sunday morning, are close together in a song or a playing style or an album or a career. The roots of R&B are buried in rewritten gospel songs and employing gospel techniques outside that genre. Soul music history is filled with people who were brought up in the Black church and went on to employ gospel tropes in secular music. Many Black artists have moved back and forth between the idioms and messages of the spiritual and the secular, trafficking in both: Marvin Gaye, Aretha Franklin, Stevie Wonder, Curtis Mayfield, Al Green, Ray Charles, Sam Cooke, James Brown, Little Richard, Whitney Houston, D'Angelo, R. Kelly, KRS-One, Lauryn Hill, Michael Jackson, and, of course, Prince, to name a few. This seems to come from many sources.

One explanation, a pragmatic view, is that music is such a large part of the Black church experience that it has become an incubator for Black musical talent. If you're born with some musical inclination and grow up hearing Black church music or singing in the choir, your talent will be developed and activated and you can't help but grow as a musician, which will impact the sort of musician you become. For many young Black people in past generations, the church was the first place they encountered or engaged in music that moved them and got public accolades for their musical talent. Another reason is that there's a deep-seated understanding in many of us that spiritual and sexual ecstasy are similar and, for some people, one urge can arise out of satisfying the other.

James Poyser, the keyboardist for the Roots, who grew up in the

Pentecostal church, told me, "As a church musician, my horniest time periods were right after I played all day on Sunday. I've spoken to quite a few preachers on this subject and they all say the spiritual/sexual nature is one and the same. Most get it in after they finish on the pulpit. Same with most gospel artists. Guess they try and keep it on the low, whereas Prince is overt about it."

Michael Eric Dyson believes the sexuality inherent in the Black church experience flows from the Black church's mission, part of which was to rescue Black people from the demonization of their bodies that was taught to them in slavery and after. In "When You Divide Body and Soul, Problems Multiply: The Black Church and Sexuality," he writes, "The rise of the black church, first as an invisible institution and then as the visible womb of black culture, provided a means of both absorbing and rejecting the sexual values of white society. Black religion freed the black body for its imprisonment in crude, racist stereotypes. The black church combated as best it could the self-hatred and the hatred of other blacks that white supremacy encouraged with evil efficiency. It fought racist oppression by becoming the headquarters of militant social and political action in black communities. The black church produced leaders who spoke with eloquence and prophetic vigor about the persistence of white racism. It was the educational center of black communities, supporting colleges that trained blacks who became shock troops in the battle for racial equality. Black churches unleashed the repressed forces of cultural creativity and religious passion. The church also redirected black sexual energies into the sheer passion and emotional explosiveness of its worship services." This, Dyson says, led to the "erotic intensity of the black worship experience: the electric call and response between minister and congregation; the fervent temper of the preacher's words of wisdom and warning; the extraordinary effort by the minister to seduce the audience onto God's side through verbal solicitation; and the orgasmic eruption of the congregation at the end of the sermon. It requires no large sophistication to tell that something like sexual stimulation was going on."[4]

Others trace the link back to Africa and the beginnings of Black music. Scholar Samuel Floyd points out in *The Power of Black Music: Interpreting Its History from Africa to the United States* that "praying had been part of the Africans' religious behavior in the homeland, and the call-and-response and ejaculatory interjections . . . were part of the African narrative and musical expressive technique . . . The preaching, praying and singing event was born of the synthesis of African religion and Christianity and it was to pervade all aspects of African-American culture, intruding into even the published music of the musically literate."[5] So, African religious traditions spawned the prayer experience of the enslaved and that developed into spirituals and/or the blues, which is the tree out of which all the rest of Black music has come.

Honorée Fanonne Jeffers, an associate professor of English at the University of Oklahoma, told me, "Both the blues and the spirituals depend upon the same twelve-bar lament and the same three-part structure of identification, exploration, and resolution. They also contain a thread of pathos—a 'blue note'—that weaves through each song, what LeRoi Jones called the 'blues feeling' in *Blues People: Negro Music in White America*. This feeling worked on and in the singer of the spirituals and the secular blues in two different ways. Spirituals are sacred songs, with their attention to worship, praise, and calls to a higher power to carry the singers, who were slaves of African descent, through hard times. The secular blues—what we know as *popular music*—contain unabashed eroticism sometimes in the form of humorous double entendres, but again, these songs are meant as artistic coping mechanisms, since the original singers of the blues were disenfranchised black folk in the segregated American South. So, essentially, the blues and the spirituals are two branches of the same tree, with one branch lifting to the divine sky, and the other pointing to the pleasure-filled earth."

Prince's music, both the profane and the spiritual, clearly derives from this blues tradition. Sometimes, he seems to be coping with the spiritual and existential crisis of "Who I am as human who will one day die and what can I do for God while I'm here and is that spreading His word or having fun and can it be both?" Sometimes he seems to be coping with the crisis of "How do I get through the days God has given me and deal with this intense desire for women" that George Clinton explained in his song "Atomic Dog," as "Why must I be like that? Why must I chase the cat? Nothin' but the dog in me." (This, even as Prince happily embraces the cat within him.) So, Prince wants to reconcile his spiritual slash religious imperative and sexual urges and seems to be searching in his music for the way to be lewdly sexual while living a righteously religious life and saying can I be both? He never gives off a whiff of guilt or shame about the marriage of sex and spirituality, which subtly says he's at peace with his two needs. He seems to be hypermodern in this desire to merge the carnality of today's world with the spirituality he holds dear but, in some ways, this is a very old concept; some pre-Christian religions considered sex a form of worship. It seems Prince does, too.

Alan Leeds told me, "For him the love of God and the sexual urges we feel are one and the same somehow. For him it all comes from the same root inside a human being. God planted these urges and it's never wrong to feel that way. The urge itself is a holy urge. Lust is a holy urge." Prince intended sexuality to be linked to the worship of God, and he filled his music with classic Christian messages, meaning Prince was sexual but, ultimately, very conservative. Eric Leeds said, "One of the last conversations I had with him, I said, ain't this a bitch. After all of these years I finally figured out what you are. You're a goddamn Republican!"

In "Sometimes It Snows In April," Prince is in mourning, but most of the time when he mentions death, especially his own, it's something he's thrilled about. A central tenet of the religious philosophy advanced in Prince's music is that death is something joyous and to be looked forward to because it means we're going to Heaven. On "Sign 'O' The Times" he says, "Some say a man ain't happy, truly, until a man truly dies." That's his philosophy of death. He believes so faithfully in resurrection and Heaven that it seems like sometimes he can't wait to die. In "Let's Go Crazy," he says, "We're all excited, but we don't know why, maybe it's cuz, we're all gonna die!" In "Controversy," he sings, "Some people wanna die, so they can be free!" He knows death is not the end but the moment of transition into the greater life. In "Reflection," on *Musicology*, he sings, "Still it's nice 2 know that, uh, when bodies wear out, we can get another." He opens *LoveSexy* with "Eye No" where he repeatedly chants, "I know there is a Heaven! I know there is a Hell!" His conviction is rock solid.

And what does the Heaven Prince envisions look like? In a 1985 *Rolling Stone* interview he says, "I think there is an afterworld. For some reason, I think it's going to be just like here."[6] But, in his songs he's much more detailed. In the "Let's Go Crazy" sermon, he describes the afterlife as, "A world of neverending happiness. You can always see the sun. Day or night." Or, does he mean you can always see the Son, as in Christ? That reading feeds into: "In this life things are much harder than the afterworld. In this life . . . you're on your own." On "The Ladder," he describes salvation as: "A feeling of self-worth will caress U. The size of the whole wide world will decrease. The love of God's creation will undress U. And time spent alone my friend, will cease." And, in "7," he adds: "There will be a new city with streets of gold. Young so educated they never grow old. And there won't be no death." This vision of heaven is why he tells us to dance in the face of impending apocalypse on "1999": even though we're about to die the best is about to come.

If you listen to Prince's entire oeuvre, the message of God's greatness and His ability to help us through the most difficult moments cannot help but seep in. In "Still Would Stand All Time," from *Graffiti Bridge*, he sings, "So many times I thought I could not make it, life was closing in, I just knew, I just knew I couldn't take it. That's when Love opened its arms." He often speaks of loneliness and posits it as the symptom for which God and Jesus are the cure. "Have U ever been so lonely that U felt U were the only one in this world?" he sings at the beginning of "Anna Stesia," on *LoveSexy*. On "Eye No," he says, "I know there was confusion, lightnin all around me. That's when I called his name. Don't U know He found me!" Later he says when He calls your name, "Your heart will thunder. U will want to hear it every day." This is interesting, coming from someone who has struggled throughout his life to find or create lasting nuclear family units, and someone who is speaking to the latchkey generation, which is particularly intimate with loneliness.

Prince often speaks of loneliness stemming from romantic abandonment; think of "Another Lonely Christmas" and "How Come U Don't Call Me Anymore" and "Nothin Compares 2 U" and "17 Days" where he says, "So here I sit in my lonely room, lookin' for my sunshine" and "Free" where he sings, "Never let that lonely monster take control of U." Prince, it seems, is finding the companionship and fulfillment that he's missing in life and love through spirituality. And he's saying to his audience that you, too, may be lonely because of family or romance and if you are you can find comfort in God. Classic preacher's message.

Touching all the bases, he also preaches about the evil side. He speaks of the anti-Christ in *Controversy*'s "Annie Christian," a sort of story song about an evil character who would have you believe, "She's His only Son." She proceeds to perpetuate much of the evil that occurs between 1980 and 1981 from the Atlanta child murders to the murder of John Lennon to the attempted murder of Ronald Reagan. In "Temptation" from *Around the World In A Day*, Prince is openly lustful until God emerges to punish him. "You have 2 want her 4 the right reasons," He tells Prince who learns "love is more important than sex." In "Let's Go Crazy," he speaks of the devil who in other songs he refers to as *Spooky Electric*.

Jesus and Satan are recurring characters in Prince's oeuvre and they're presented in traditional ways. However, he doesn't share rock's classic sympathy for the devil. He wants to stamp out Satan and get as many people as possible to follow Christ.

Sometimes he buries the message. In "1999," Prince sings, "I got a lion in my pocket and baby he's ready to roar." This seems like a sexual reference, saying, beside dancing he's also ready to screw, but it may be a Biblical reference. A religious scholar pointed out this verse in Peter: "Be of sober spirit, be on the alert. Your adversary, the devil, prowls around like a roaring lion, seeking someone to devour." So, the lion in Prince's pocket may signify the devil, as in he's got the devil under control. Then again, Revelation speaks of the Lion of Judah, a symbol for Christ. Perhaps the lion is a reference to Jesus as in Prince saying Christ is with him.

Jason Hines, a longtime Adventist who is a Harvard Law grad and a PhD candidate in Church–State Studies at Baylor, told me, "If Prince is trying to get us to accept a new religious paradigm, that paradigm would have to be that religion is fun, as evidenced in the voice of God at the beginning of the song. If religion is supposed to be a party, if spirituality is not supposed to have us running in fear, then referencing the lion could mean Prince's approach to religion. When Prince says 'If U didn't come 2 party / Don't bother knockin' on my door / I got a lion in my pocket / And baby he's ready 2 roar' is it possible Prince is making an allusion to evangelism? Mentioning door knocking makes me think he might be saying, 'If you're coming with that old, dry, sad, afraid, religion that makes people scared then don't knock on my door with that.' If that's where Prince is going, then the next line has to be a Christ reference. Prince would be saying that he already has Christ with him, the lion of Judah in his pocket, and that lion is getting ready to change the way we do things (in terms of spirituality and religious expression)." Hines said we must assume Prince is deeply familiar with the Bible because there's evidence of it throughout his work.

Prince wasn't just preaching to his audience: He needed to see the spirit in those who worked for him. "When he hired people," Alan Leeds said, "there was some point in the first month or so of your employ that he'd catch you in the cafeteria or in the tour bus or some-place where it just happened to be the two of you and out of nowhere he's gonna look at you and say, Do you believe in God? And I always thought that was a litmus test, and depending on your answer, you may or may not have a job tomorrow.

A person's relationship with God may have signified to Prince their level of maturity. In a 1985 *Rolling Stone* interview, he said, "I think when one discovers himself he discovers God. Or maybe it's the other way around."[7] This is echoed in these lines from "Anna Stesia": "Maybe I could learn 2 love, if I was just closer 2 somethin', closer to your higher self, I don't know, closer to Heaven, closer to God." In that *Rolling Stone* interview, he also described his home as "a shrine to Jesus, love and peace."[8] In 1998, when I interviewed Prince he told me, "If you don't have a relationship with God, you're in trouble. That gives you something to put everything in line."

LoveSexy is Prince's most evangelical album during his zenith. He told Eric Leeds that the term *LoveSexy* means, "God is love. God loves you," but that doesn't fully account for the word *sex* and the clear attempt to try to merge spirituality and sexuality, and positing that they go hand in hand and emerge from the same place in the soul. Alan Leeds said, "The explanation for *Lovesexy* [the word] that I got was that they're one and the same."

Eric Leeds told me that Prince considered *LoveSexy* his most personal album because he was trying to explain his philosophy. That's why *LoveSexy* was sequenced as a single track, forcing us to listen to it in the order intended, so we would get Prince's messages. Leeds explained that Prince was saying, "This is how you're gonna have to listen to it because I want you to be sure to understand what this album is about and the only way that you can understand what this album is about is you can't choose what you want to listen to and what you don't, you're gonna have to listen to the whole damn thing."

LoveSexy begins with "Eye No," when he contrasts the effects of following Satan and the word of God: "I know there is a devil because he talks so loud. He makes U do things that your friends do, hang out with the crowd." The singing there is a bit jumbled and words overlap as if to simulate cognitive overload. Then, suddenly, everything slows and calms and is peaceful: "But my Lord, He is so quiet." In *LoveSexy*'s title song he speaks of the feeling of having God within you, singing, "This feelings's so good in every single way! I want it morning, noon and night of every day!" He says he must spread the word: "And I got 2 tell the world. I just can't keep it to myself! All in life becomes easier. No question is unresolved. And I'm not afraid."

He concludes "Anna Stesia" singing, "Save me Jesus, I've been a fool. How could I forget that U are the rule. U are my God, I am Your child. From now on, 4 U I shall be wild! I shall be quick! I shall be strong! I'll tell Your story! No matter how long . . . ! We're just a play in Your master plan. Now, my Lord, I understand." In "Positivity," the last song on *LoveSexy*, he sings of "Spooky Electric," "In every man's life there will be a hang-up, a whirlwind designed 2 slow U down. It cuts like a knife and tries 2 get in U. This Spooky Electric sound." The next lines are crucial. "Give up if U want 2 and all is lost. Spooky Electric will be your boss." Then he explains what happens if evil becomes your leader—next thing you know you'll be holding "a .57 mag with the price tag still on the side." The alternative is: "U can fly high right by Spooky and all that he crawls 4."

The *LoveSexy* tour further played out Prince's desire to evangelize. Woodworth told me it was Prince's "most direct enactment of the death and transfiguration of Christ." The show was split into two halves. The first half gave us songs with an overtly sexual component like "Head," "Erotic City," "Sister," and "Dirty Mind." Alan Leeds and Matt Fink said Prince knew that's what people wanted; he was luring them in, so that he can then discuss what he really wants them to hear. Just before the midpoint, he did "Bob George" from the *Black Album*, perhaps his most misogynistic song, one where he insults himself and masculinity, one that represents the depths of evil which the *Black Album* represented for him. This we can read as the moment of hell just before death in Adventist theology. It's his always-darkest-before-dawn moment. He would symbolically die and then be reborn by going into "Anna Stesia," which gives us spirituality, as he sings, "liberate my mind." As he did the song, he was behind a keyboard on a riser that lifted him higher and higher as he was bathed in a pinpoint spotlight. Near the end of the song, he would twitch and convulse as he ascended into the light acting out a physical conversion. Once again, he is Jesuslike.

After that, the band would go into a vamp and Prince would preach. Matt Fink said, "He would stop in the middle of the show and we would hang out for a good ten minutes or so on stage playing a bit of music real quiet while he would be preaching to the audience. Literally." This would lead them into the second half of the show filled with uplifting, positive, Christian-inspired music from *LoveSexy*, marking his resurrection or rebirth. Eric Leeds told me, "The whole point of the show was I'm going to do the dirty half of me in the first half because that's what you came to hear, but [in] the second half I'm gonna show you what it's really supposed to be about."

LoveSexy meant so much to Prince that its lack of commercial success really hurt him. "When that album flopped he took it very personally," Eric said. "He went through a crisis of conscience and confidence about his place in popular music." Alan Leeds told me, "It was his first real failure." The commercial disappointment had little to do with *LoveSexy* being an overtly religious album and more to do with the album's cover, featuring a picture of Prince nude, which led to several big box retailers refusing to sell it, as well as the CD being released as one continuous song that didn't allow easy skipping around, which annoyed critics, radio DJs, and fans. On top of this, against all advice, Prince decided to scrap a planned US tour at the last minute and went to Europe instead. By the time he got back to performing in America, his lack of visibility here had doused whatever hype there had been for *LoveSexy*, depressing record sales and ticket sales.

Alan Leeds explained, "The *LoveSexy* tour receipts fell significantly below expectations. There wasn't the demand for extended runs that was expected in 'A' markets and some small-market shows failed to sell out." Of course, none of this would deter Prince from going on to make more religious music, like 1992's *The Symbol* album and 2001's *Rainbow Children*, which reflects his becoming a Jehovah's Witness.

Prince's 1980s compatriot in bringing religious iconography into the pop arena was Madonna. She was iconoclastic, challenging conventions and attacking respect for old ways. Madonna's message was be whoever you want to be: Identity is fungible and mutable and as changeable as clothes. And, whatever you do, don't listen to the older generation; they don't know what they're talking about. She was relentlessly subversive, wearing a cross and referencing religion in order to shock, because it made her even more of a bad girl and attracted gen Xers, who appreciated her thumbing her nose at the old guard. In the video for "Like A Prayer" she imagines herself getting stigmata, dances in front of burning crosses, and dreams of being sexual with a saint, who is Black—a parade of heretical gestures. She's like a sardonic sinner dancing blasphemously in church to show up the whole ritual.

Prince's message was different in many ways: He was extremely and seriously religious, so deeply so that spirituality remained part of him during his most sexual moments. He would never present himself making fun of religious rituals in a video; he was too devout for that. Where Madonna said screw all the rules, Prince preached about old, traditional rules that come from Christian doctrine. The metamessage in his music wasn't one typically heard in pop: It wasn't countercultural, it wasn't rebellious, it wasn't rejecting everything your parents believe in. It was: Religion matters. Christ is the way. There is a Heaven and a Hell, a God and a Satan, and Judgment Day is coming, get ready! Death is the portal to the afterlife. Sex is not a sin; it's part of loving humanity and God. And loving God is essential. We must love and follow Christ and spread the word of how great he is.

"The guy has a very provincial, evangelical attitude toward the world," Alan Leeds said. "He really believes in sin and that God is gonna punish us and blow this shit up. He really believes that. Now, there's a point in his life where he's like yeah, that's gonna happen, but this shit is fun, so I'm gonna roll with it. And I'm gonna make dirty songs." Questlove noted the same struggle. "He had this conflicted core about wanting to be the poster child for hedonism as a career move and on the other hand having this deep-seated sense that consequence is a real thing from a spiritual perspective. It's like that line from *Gladiator*: 'What we do in life echoes in eternity.' And he did wrestle with that personally."

Prince is now a Jehovah's Witness, but he converted later in life, in 2001. During the hottest period of his career he claimed no religious affiliation, but his music is filled with end-time religious prophecy and gospel tropes, which seem to stem from his childhood when he attended Baptist church services and Methodist church camp but, primarily, was raised a Seventh-day Adventist, often attending service with his grandmother at Glendale Seventh-day Adventist Church in Minneapolis. Both of his parents believed in the strict faith as did Bernadette Anderson, who took him in after he left home. The teachings and iconography of Adventism show up repeatedly in Prince's music, which I didn't understand until I spoke with several Seventh-day Adventists. Interestingly, both Adventists and Jehovah's Witnesses are known as end-time movements, which use the Bible as a source of prophecy with encoded information about the future apocalypse, so it's not a large intellectual leap for Prince to become a Jehovah's Witness after a childhood in Adventism.

Prince told Chris Rock, "I was made to go to church when I was young. Most thing I got out of that is the experience of the choir." This is interesting because all the Adventists I spoke with said music is a crucial part of the Black SDA experience. One said, "Music is the foundation of how Black SDAs worship." Another said, "Black SDAs are rooted in their mastery of music—most Blacks in SDA are musically inclined and there's a strong emphasis on music. The development of musical talent and ability is taken very seriously."

The list of successful SDA musicians includes: Little Richard, Kirk Franklin, Brian McKnight, and Pepa from Salt 'N' Pepa. This would have been mother's milk to the boy who was always fascinated by music. In 1984, Mattie Shaw told the *Minneapolis Star Tribune*, "When he was three or four, we'd go to the department store and he'd jump on the radio, the organ, any type of instrument there was. Mostly the piano and organ. I'd have to hunt for him and that's where'd be— in the music department."

Prince also told Chris Rock that, once the sermonizing began, he didn't like much of what he heard. "As far as a message was concerned," Prince explained, "a lot of it was based in fear, what will happen to you if you do something and I don't think God is to be feared that way. I think he's a loving God." However, a close listen to Prince's music conducted with an understanding of Adventist teaching, reveals that he must have been listening to the sermons because he took their messages into his career.

The Adventist church was born after a prediction of the Second Coming of Christ in 1844. When Christ did not return, many people were crushed—it's called the *Great Disappointment*—and they returned to their Bibles to figure out where they had gone wrong. Many concluded that the Second Coming was indeed imminent and they needed to be prepared. The SDA ideology was developed by people who thought the prediction was not altogether wrong and that going forward they had to be in constant readiness for the arrival of Christ. Jason Hines explained, "The Great Disappointment is part of the Adventists' denominational DNA." Further, "There is a strong emphasis in Adventism on getting the prophecies correct." He said that prophecies of Revelation and the ever-imminent return of Christ figure prominently in Adventist theology.

Another lifelong Adventist told me, "Growing up, Prince would've heard the world was going to end any day now and you had to keep constant watch." This perhaps explains why Prince's music is so often concerned with the apocalypse and the Second Coming and unveils the real meaning of the refrain "May you live to see the dawn." This also speaks to why he seems to be evangelical, using his music to spread a message about Christ.

In "1999," Prince writes, "This morning when I woke up coulda sworn it was Judgment Day." The proximity of armageddon in this vision is very Adventist. This gives new color, perhaps, to the lines, "Tryin' to run from the destruction. You know I didn't even care." If Prince is looking forward to Judgment Day, then it'd make sense that he'd be sitting pretty, ready to go to Heaven, while others are running scared. So, in "1999," Prince sees others running from the apocalypse because they don't know better, or because they fear death, but Prince doesn't run, and isn't afraid because he knows what's happening and he welcomes the end of days. He knows death is the portal to Heaven.

In Adventist theology, the dead do not go to Heaven right away. An Adventist said the common phrase that a dead person is looking down from Heaven would mean nothing to an Adventist, and Prince tends not to use that language. They believe that, upon death, we go into a soul sleep which lasts until Christ returns, at which point all souls will be resurrected and go en masse to Heaven. One Adventist told me, "We don't believe people just die and go to the pearly gates. They rest and wait." So, the apocalypse described in "1999" would not be frightening for Prince, but could be thrilling; now here's the Judgment Day that signals the moment for all of us to go to Heaven. He sings, "Can't run from Revelation, no," and he doesn't want to.

Many Adventists believe that Judgment Day will be accompanied or preceded by war. The downward spiral of society is a typically Adventist perspective. They believe the world will get much worse before the Second Coming and that the return of Christ will usher in a millennium of peace. Religious scholars use the term *premillenialist* to describe the belief of religions, like Adventism, that the world will get worse before Jesus returns. The premillenialist perspective fits with Prince's dour, hopeless, pessimistic, look-at-the-messed-up-world songs like "America," "Pop Life," and "Sign 'O' The Times." Interestingly, there's a popular Adventist magazine named *Signs of the Times.* Their tagline is, "Encouraging readers to lead joyful Christian lives as they await the soon return of Jesus." It's curious that Prince gave us an album that shares the name of an Adventist magazine, with a title track that speaks of the end of days scenario that would precede the return of Jesus in Prince's theology. Then, he goes to work on the *Black Album.* He got through it quickly, having recorded some of it while making *Sign "O" the Times.* The last song he recorded was the sweet "When 2 R In Love," which was an omen for the music that would be recorded next and form *LoveSexy.*

After the *Black Album* was completed, Prince went to dinner with singer Ingrid Chavez, who was his girlfriend at the time. Alan Leeds said, "Speculation is they shared some mushrooms or ecstasy and by middle of the night slash very early morning he was calling Karen, his personal assistant, offering mushy apologies for ever addressing her rudely. Totally out of character. Then instructed her to call any and everyone she could muster to make sure the album was stopped. It was literally due to ship within twenty-four hours. Later, his only explanation to us was he had a vision that he died and the *Black Album* would have been his legacy and he didn't want something he now viewed as 'negative' to be that." Afterward, he pivots 180 degrees to create his most openly spiritual album to that point, *LoveSexy.*

All the Adventists I spoke with said one Prince song employs far more SDA language than any other: "7," from the *Symbol* album. "It's about the end of times," one told me. "It is exactly what we have been taught from a young age." Hines said that Adventism founder Ellen G. White, who is believed by the faithful to have had authentic visions from God, wrote forty books, including one called *The Great Controversy*, which speaks of the Second Coming and what will follow it. White's book prophesied that, after the Second Coming, the saints will go to Heaven and reign with Christ for one thousand years, then return to the Earth and reign in the New Jerusalem. That's when Satan would form an army to attack the city. They would fail, be destroyed, and a new, sin-free universe would be established. Hines explaines, "SDAs believe that after the millennium, the New Jerusalem will come to Earth from Heaven and that hellfire will kill the wicked. It seems that what Prince describes in '7' is particularly in line with Adventist eschatology. The entirety of Prince's '7' is a description of this final battle."

In "7"'s chorus, we hear of the forces aligned with Satan, and White's certainty that the Army of God will defeat them: "They stand

in the way of love. And we will smoke them all." Hines notes that the
first verse begins by alluding to the song as a vision: "And I saw an
angel come down unto me." He said visions are often sent by angels.
This, in my opinion, is more of Prince presenting himself as prophetic.
In this vision, Prince sees or hears "an Army's marching feet," which
refers to the army Satan is using to attack the New Jerusalem. Prince
then says that they "lay down on the sand of the sea." Hines said he
may be talking about laying on the shore by the sea of glass, which is
said to be in the heavenly city. Then, Prince says, "Before us animosity
will stand and decree that we speak not of love, only blasphemy, and
in the distance six others will curse me." This is Satan's army being evil,
lying about them, and cursing them.

Other Adventists said the second verse is quite common in their
teaching: "And we will see a plague and a river of blood." This is classic
Christian imagery—the plague and the river of blood are mentioned
in Revelation. "And every evil soul will surely die in spite of their seven
tears." Thus, the battle with Satan's army has been won. Prince goes on
to describe the eternal life they will have: "Do not fear four in the distance, twelve souls from now, u and me will still be here." One Adventist told me, "Man, how many times have we been told that. Totally
SDA." Woodworth noticed that the Exodus imagery referenced in "7"
is matched by the *Symbol* album's imagery which places the characters in an imagined ancient Egypt. He said, "Prince weaves Egyptian
imagery throughout the Symbol album, from the cover shot of the
pyramids to his use of belly-dancing imagery and in '7' even drops in
a brief modal guitar riff at 3:06, a 'snake-charmer' moment, that sonically recalls Egypt or, at least, the Middle East. The listener is meant
to feel that this sonic landscape is somehow in the lands of the Bible."

Not incidentally, Prince has shown an obsessive affinity for the
number 7 throughout his career from the song "7" to "it's been seven
hours" since she's been gone in "Nothing Compares 2 U" to it's been

"seven years" since his lover died in "Another Lonely Christmas" to "Let's Pretend We're Married" where he asks if she "ain't busy for the next seven years" to he's epileptic till the age of 7 on the *Symbol* album's "Sacrifice of Victor" to it's 7:45 at the beginning of "Starfish and Coffee" to "if I see eleven, you can say it's seven," in "I Wish You Heaven" to "Reflection from Musicology" which begins "two seven's together, like time indefinite," to "I Love U In Me" where he begs for a kiss and she gives him seven to "My Name Is Prince," where he says God made him on the seventh day. This extends with the song "17 days" and the song "Mountains" where he speaks of seventeen mountains and "Tambourine" where he references trolley cars that juggle seventeen and "Sign 'O' the Times" where seventeen-year-old boys are gang members and even "Alphabet Street" where he says he's gonna drive his Daddy's Thunderbird which is either a '66 or a '67. There's also an instrumental on 2009's *Lotusflow3r* called "77 Beverly Park" and a song Prince wrote for The Time called "777-9311" and the 2004 album *3121* whose numbers add up to . . . This is not a trifle. This is a reference to the number seven as a symbol of completion or perfection. God finished the world in seven days. In Hebrew, *seven* is derived from a word meaning to be complete or full. The number appears in the Bible more abundantly than any other number, just as it appears in Prince's oeuvre more than any other number.

Conclusion

Pᴿᴵɴᴄᴇ ꜱᴛᴀʀᴛᴇᴅ ᴀꜱ ᴀ ʜʏᴘᴇʀꜱᴇxᴜᴀʟ trickster bragging of having a dirty mind, telling everyone he was a musical lothario but, over time, he more and more used his music as a way to spread the word of God and painted himself as a Messiah symbol. He did not become famous, and then introduce his spirituality—he rose to megastardom largely on the strength of hits with spiritual messages—"Controversy," "1999," "Let's Go Crazy," "Purple Rain," and "I Would Die 4 U." It's almost as if he's being rewarded for fulfilling a spiritual imperative in the audience. Or, as several people said, he was looking to God to explain his many blessings.

Alan Leeds, who was tour manager for James Brown, Prince, and D'Angelo, said, "I've been around a lot of artists, including several icons, and I've never seen anybody like Prince. He's a freak of nature in terms of how the music flowed through him. The gift that allowed him to pick up any instrument and figure it out quickly to the point where he's not really playing the instrument, it's just music coming through him through the instrument, it's just part of that funnel from whatever this source is and you can't separate his work from his spirituality. And I think Prince really does think he's special. I've always believed that he thinks he has an in with God. Where that comes from is that this is a guy who sits there and says how in the world did someone like me get the gift I have? Where does that come from? Because the level of his gift is spooky. I've been around a lot of brilliantly creative people, from Miles Davis to James Brown to D'Angelo, and I've never seen anyone who's a vessel for music the way Prince was. He'd be trying to sleep because he hasn't slept in two days and he can't because he's gotta write down lyrics, and then it's can you find me a studio, I gotta get this out. Gotta get it out. Gotta get it on tape. Once it's on tape, it's out, and then I can sleep. It was crazy. I've never seen anything like it. And you can't say, Well, Prince there's a studio in the next town and we've got a day off . . . Nah, I gotta get it out. His every waking moment there was music or lyrics flowing to a piece of paper. If he doesn't have anything to do he'll go to the studio. He wakes up in the morning with a melody or a lyric and he can't wait to get to the studio to turn the tape on. You just wondered how any one brain could process as much music came out of him. All of it wasn't good. But enough of it was. I mean, there's a lot of good guitar players. There's a lot of good singers. There's a lot of great songwriters. He's all of that. For a lot of artists it's what they do. For him, it's not what he does; it's who he is. You cannot divide Prince from the music. That's why he plays aftershows to the point of exhaustion. Because he has to play. To the point of obsession that's borderline sick. It's like goddamn, don't your fingers get tired? Don't you wanna watch a ballgame? It's crazy. And I think he sat there and decided God anointed me."

    In a 1985 interview with the legendary Detroit radio DJ Electrifying Mojo, Prince talked about his seemingly inexhaustible work ethic and said, "The thing is that when you're called, you're called. I hear things in my sleep; I walk around and go to the bathroom and try to brush my teeth and all of the sudden the toothbrush starts vibrating! That's a groove!"[1] It's telling, I think, that he refers to musical inspiration as *being called*. While I was working on my 1998 story, Prince emailed me this: "Ultimately, spiritual evolution is the axis on which inspiration and creativity spin . . . there r so many songs that I've written and recorded, sometimes it is hard 4 ME 2 believe it comes from one source!" And, intriguingly, "All of my musicality comes from GOD . . . the blessing/curse ensued when I kept sneaking back in2 the talent line dressed as another person . . . I got away with it several times be4 they caught me!!"

An old girlfriend said that Prince doesn't always welcome the never-ending flow of music. "He has no control over his life," she told me. "The music is channeled through him. When the music tells him to play, he does. When the music tells him to sleep, he does. He considers it a blessing and a curse." Still, it's Prince's intense relationship with music that leads him to think he has an unusually close relationship with God. He has no say over the flow of music, so he feels that it must be coming from a higher power. And that is the source of him thinking of himself as celestially special. Unless, it's a way of making sense of his extreme professional success.

"I think that he felt especially fortunate and that [his relationship with God] was really good coping mechanism," Susan Rogers said. "I think he felt especially blessed. I mean, how does someone make that journey? How do you make that journey from being nobody, from being in a family that's not well known, they have no money, they have no fame, they have no great accomplishment. How do you leap over everyone you know into a brand-new world of wealth and fame and recognition? How does that make sense in your world? What allows you to be so special and not Morris Day, not Jesse Johnson, not Sheila E., or any of the other talented people you know? What do you attribute that to? I think in order to remain sane you have to recognize that there has to be a causal factor and I think it's probably crazy as hell to attribute that causal factor to something that was internal, because then you could lose it. If it's coming from you and you lose yourself, everything is lost. But, if your power, your strength is coming from an external source, then it can still be there when you lose your will or you lose your way. I think in order to be a successful artist in any field there is a strong element of madness. You have to have this deep well of creativity and you have to have the madness of the artist. But you won't be successful unless that can balanced against the sanity and reason of the rational man or woman and Prince was extraordinary, I mean extraordinary in his capacity to take this deep well of creativity and true madness, the madness that is genius and live with it in a sane, successful way. It's almost unprecedented. I mean, at least in the last half of the twentieth century. If we look at Michael Jackson and Madonna and other people, they either didn't have the talent that he did, in the case of Madonna, or they didn't have the sanity that he did, in the case of Michael Jackson. There are other examples of people who just go off the rails from being that gifted and he hasn't, more or less he hasn't. So, I think that he doesn't see himself as God or Jesus but he certainly had to psychologically see himself as favored, I would assume."

Many of Prince's songs have nothing to do with religious or spiritual messages, because that is not his sole interest and would not have led to him becoming the rock star he dreamed of becoming. But, more than that, for him sex and religion are symbiotic: He believed that sex was part of worship and lust came from God so it can't be wrong. He's interested in both Saturday night and Sunday morning and he's able to move between both and to somehow pull them closer together. However, there's so much Sunday morning in his music that, when you take stock of his career, I wonder if it wasn't, on some deeper level, really about proselytizing.

Prince's focus on religion is so much more persistent and enthusiastic than his focus on sex. When you look at how often and how passionately he talks about Jesus and God and religion and spirituality, his oeuvre reveals itself as a form of evangelizing. The man thought early on that he was here to spread a message. Surely, that message couldn't have been have wilder sex. No, he seems to have used portraying pure sex as a lure, or maybe a sort of loss leader: Something meant to get you into the store, no matter the cost to the store, so they can sell you the things they really want to sell you. It was like hiding vitamins in chocolate cake. He made a conscious decision to portray pure sex and get a rise out of people to earn him attention, because he was a calculating marketing genius, but what was he going to do with that attention because he knew music was meant to serve a much higher purpose. As he told Chris Rock, "Music was put on earth to enlighten and empower us and feel closer to our center."[2] He seems to have tried to live up to that and as he grew up and found himself as a spiritual being, and grew in his ability to express God through his music, he gave us more and more of that part of himself.

The lyric that may best sum up Prince's career is, "We are gathered here today to get through this thing called *life*." We are together, listening to his music inside the virtual Holy Church of Prince as a way to help us cope with this earthly stage that we refer to as *life* but is not the real life. Prince's message was pitch perfect for gen X but, at the same time, it was thousands of years old and has worked on every continent and in every era that has embraced Christianity. And thus, the Kid, who cultivated a reputation for sexual deviance, eventually unveiled himself as the most important religious artist ever. Not the best, but the one who had the greatest impact on people, because he was a crossover megastar spreading the word to millions who would normally reject a gospel record or a Christian message. He was not preaching to the choir, unlike most gospel artists. He was outside the church on the street, preaching to people who didn't hear him coming as he put spiritual messages in their head. Jesus ministered to the least, the last, and the lost; He sat with prostitutes and lepers. In a way, Prince did the same by taking his spiritual message to the pop world, to the uninitiated.

Imagine America as one house on a suburban lane. Years before he became a Jehovah's Witness, Prince knocked on America's door through his music. He came to the door holding a guitar and an umbrella while concealing a Bible. He flirted his way inside the door and told us he had a dirty mind and was controversial, and then he sat down in the living room on the good couch. And, when America's guard was down, because we thought we were having a conversation about sex, Prince eased out his Bible and said, let me also tell you about my Lord and savior, Jesus Christ.

Notes

Introduction

1. Alex Hahn, *Possessed: The Rise and Fall of Prince* (New York: Billboard Books, 2003).
2. "Prince: An Oral History," *Minneapolis Star Tribune*, March 14, 2004.
3. Hahn, *Possessed*.

Chapter One: Prince's Rosebud

1. Kurt Loder, "Jagger in Conversation," *Rolling Stone*, November, 24, 1983.
2. The *Oprah Winfrey Show*, "The Artist Formerly Known as Prince," November 21, 1996.
3. Barbara Graostark, "Prince Talks," *Musician*, September 1983.
4. Jon Bream, *Prince: Inside the Purple Reign* (New York: Scribner, 1984).
5. VH1 interview with Chris Rock, 1998.
6. Ellen Zoe Golden, "Prince: The Controversial Interview," *Rock & Soul*, June 1983.
7. Dave Hill, *Prince: A Pop Life*, Harmony Books, 1989.
8. Jeffrey Jolson-Colburn, Prince, and Andre Cymone, "Stardom and Conflict," *Rock*, April, 1984.
9. Michelle Green, "The Sexy Enigma of Rock Makes a Royal Statement in His Debut Film *Purple Rain*," *People*, August 20, 1984.

10. Alan and Gwen Leeds, "Behind the Purple Rain, Prince and the Revolution," *Wax Poetics*, Winter 2012.
11. Lynn Norment, "Prince: Story Behind Passion for Purple, Privacy," *Ebony*, November 1984.
12. Neal Karlen, "Prince Talks," *Rolling Stone*, April 26, 1985.
13. Ibid.
14. Hill, *Prince: A Pop Life*.
15. Jon Bream, " 'Purple Rain' Debut Shows Hollywood Who Prince Is," *Minneapolis Star Tribune*, July 27, 1984.
16. Jon Bream, "Prince's Mom Passes Away at 68," *Minneapolis Star Tribune*, February 20, 2002.
17. Ibid.
18. Michelle Green, "The Sexy Enigma of Rock Makes a Royal Statement in His Debut Film *Purple Rain*."
19. Hill, *Prince: A Pop Life*.
20. Bream, *Prince: Inside the Purple Reign*.
21. "Prince: An Oral History."
22. Green, "The Sexy Enigma of Rock Makes a Royal Statement in His Debut Film *Purple Rain*."
23. "Prince An Oral History."
24. Jeff Giles, "Generalization X," *Newsweek*, June 6, 1994.

Chapter Two: The King of Porn Chic

1. Pauline Kael, "The Charismatic Half and Halfs," *The New Yorker*, August 20, 1984.
2. Bill Adler, "Will the Little Girls Understand?" *Rolling Stone*, February 19, 1981. This is from Bill Adler's notes and not in the original story.
3. Griffin Woodworth, "Just Another One of God's Gifts: Prince, African-American Masculinity and the Sonic Legacy of the Eighties" (Ph.D. diss., University of California, Los Angeles, 1984).
4. Stan Hawkins and Sarah Niblock, *Prince: The Making of a Pop Music Phenomenon* (Farnham, UK: Ashgate, 2011).
5. Davis Guggenheim, *From the Sky Down* (BBC Worldwide Canada, 2011), film.
6. Pers Nilsen, *Dance Music Sex Romance: Prince: The First Decade* (London: SAF Publishing, 2003).
7. Alex Hahn, *Possessed: The Rise and Fall Of Prince* (New York: Billboard Books, 2003).

8. Bill Adler, "Will the Little Girls Understand?"
9. "Prince: An Oral History," *Minneapolis Star Tribune*, March 14, 2004.
10. Hahn, *Possessed.*
11. Jon Bream, *Prince: Inside the Purple Reign* (New York: Scribner, 1984).

Chapter Three: I'm Your Messiah

1. Dave Hill, *Prince: A Pop Life* (New York: Harmony Books, 1989).
2. VH1 interview with Chris Rock, 1998.
3. Griffin Woodworth, "Just Another One of God's Gifts: Prince, African-American Masculinity and the Sonic Legacy of the Eighties" (Ph.D. diss., University of California, Los Angeles, 1984).
4. Michael Eric Dyson, "When You Divide Body and Soul, Problems Multiply: The Black Church and Sexuality," *Race Rule: Navigating the Color Line* (Reading, MA: Addison-Wesley, 1996).
5. Samuel Floyd, *The Power of Black Music: Interpreting Its History from Africa to the United States* (New York: Oxford University Press, 1995).
6. Neal Karlen, "Prince Talks," *Rolling Stone*, April 26, 1985.
7. Ibid.
8. Ibid.

Conclusion

1. Interview with Electrifying Mojo, WHYT, June 6, 1985.
2. VH1 interview with Chris Rock, 1998.

Acknowledgments

Skip Gates for starting me on this journey, Questlove, Alan Leeds, Jason Silverstein, Ian Jackson, Prince Vault, and, of course, Rita, Hendrix, and Fairuz.

Index

About the Author

Touré is a co-host of MSNBC's *The Cycle* and a columnist for Time .com. He is the author of *Who's Afraid of Post-Blackness?*, a *New York Times* and *Washington Post* notable book. He is the author of three other books. He lives in Brooklyn with his wife and two kids. Follow @Toure on Twitter.